D1077025

# Improving the Care of Elderly People with Mental Health Problems: Clinical Audit Project Examples

Guild Community Healt'
NHS Trust
Medical Library Guild
Academic Centre
Royal Preston Hospital

ACCESSION
NUMBER  5366

CLASSIFICATION
NUMBER  WT 150

**DATE DUE**

| | | |
|---|---|---|
| 31 OCT 2002 | | |
| 1 6 DEC 2008 | | |
| 2 6 NOV 2009 | | |
| 3 0 SEP 2010 | | |
| 10 Jun 2011 | | |
| | | |
| | | |
| | | |
| | | |
| | | |
| | | |
| | | |
| | | |
| | | |
| | | |
| GAYLORD | | PRINTED IN U.S.A. |

WITHDRAWN

# Improving the Care of Elderly People with Mental Health Problems: Clinical Audit Project Examples

Kirsty MacLean Steel and Claire Palmer

LIBRARY AND INFORMATION SERVICE
YORK DISTRICT HOSPITAL
YORK
YO31 8HE

Published by Gaskell
London

© The Royal College of Psychiatrists 1999.

Gaskell is an imprint and registered trade mark of the Royal College of Psychiatrists, 17 Belgrave Square, London SW1X 8PG

All rights reserved. No part of this book may be reprinted or reproduced or utilised in any form or by any electronic, mechanical, or other means, now known or hereafter invented, including photocopying and recording, or in any information storage or retrieval system, without permission in writing from the publishers.

**British Library Cataloguing-in-Publication Data**
A catalogue record for this book is available from
the British Library.
ISBN 1-901242-38-2


Distributed in North America
by American Psychiatric Press, Inc.
ISBN 0-88048-971-5

The views presented in this book do not necessarily reflect
those of the Royal College of Psychiatrists, and the publishers
are not responsible for any error of omission or fact.


The Royal College of Psychiatrists is a registered charity (no. 228636).

Printed by Bell & Bain Limited, Thornliebank, Glasgow.

# Contents

## The clinical audit projects

### Referrals

### Assessment

### Care plans

### Medication

### Clinical care

## Depression/Deliberate self-harm/Suicide

## Organisational/management processes

## Discharge

# Foreword

Clinical audit is the key tool with which we can look at the service we provide and measure it against standards set, derived from evidence of best practice. It is clear in the National Health Service today that best practice in any one area may not be able to reach 'gold standards' because of resource implications. By using audit, however, we can see where we are at and identify the nature of any lack of resources. This lack is not always money – often it is a particular skill or simply an inefficiency in a particular area. Measuring the gap between reality and gold standards gives us the opportunity to establish information on what we can do to improve practice where possible, but also to inform ourselves (and our patients and commissioners) when and why it is not within our ability to reach these standards. Information collated in this way is a powerful tool for negotiation when changes are being discussed at senior management level.

Some argue that such standards do not exist in many areas, or that they are inadequate. In fact, the research base in old age psychiatry is increasingly rich and the field is continually changing and growing. Opportunities for clinical audit are therefore endless. This book is an excellent collection of clinical audit projects on varied topics, which shows examples of standards set against evidence and locally agreed standards. These examples give a good feel for what is being achieved and, for many of us, will act as useful tools to implement in our own practice, or to generate ideas of our own. Thus, collections of this sort can help to promote good practice. In addition, we can begin to set new standards as the examples aggregate. In this way, the speciality of old age psychiatry can set goals and aim to achieve equality for our patients across the UK.

Clinical audit is not research, and therefore can be done by anybody. It is a measurement of what we do and a key element of clinical governance. We must do it ourselves, on ourselves, and be honest. One hundred per cent compliance with standards is gratifying and reassuring but does not change practice. We learn from the shortfalls and need to be brave enough to admit them. The examples presented here show the changes (often simple ones) with which practice has improved. Our speciality is new – its prospects look bright. I hope the next edition of this book is twice the size.

Dr Roger Bullock
Consultant in Old Age Psychiatry
October 1998

# Acknowledgements

We thank the following people for their invaluable help: Dr David N. Anderson and Dr Roger Bullock from the Royal College of Psychiatrist's Old Age Faculty and Victoria Thomas and Sam Coombs at the Royal College of Psychiatrists' Research Unit.

We are also indebted to the following contributors for their help and generosity in sharing their work with us:

Gaynor Abbott, Thameside Community Healthcare NHS Trust

A. J. Hadi Al-Barazanchi, South Buckinghamshire NHS Trust

Jane Bemrose, Bridlington and District Hospital, Yorkshire

Paula Bramley, Riverside Mental Health Trust, London

Robert Chaplin, Tooting and Furzedown Community Mental Health Trust

Robert Colgate, Glanrhyd Hospital, Wales

Peter J. Connelly, Murray Royal Hospital, Perth

C. Gorst-Unsworth, Memorial Hospital, London

Gina James, Mental Health Services of Salford NHS Trust

Helen Leegood, Chichester Priority Care Services NHS Trust

Susan Logie, Sunnyside Royal Hospital, Tayside

Ann Marshall, Newtown House, Hampshire

Russell Mason, St Clements Hospital, Ipswich

Ruth McDonald, Homefirst Community Trust, County Antrim

Michael Philpot, Maudsley Hospital, London

Jackie Pile, East Wiltshire Health Care NHS Trust

Henry Rosenvinge, Moorgreen Hospital, Southampton

Ruth Saffrey, South Birmingham Mental Health NHS Trust

Wendy Searle, Severn NHS Trust

A. K. Shah, West London NHS Healthcare Trust

Austyn Snowden, Bridlington and District Hospital, Yorkshire

Graham Stokes, Premier Health NHS Trust, Staffordshire

R. I. Tobiansky, Colindale Hospital, London

Sara Turner, Pathfinder Mental Health Services NHS Trust, London

Sylvia Warwick, Fair Mile Hospital, Oxfordshire

Sharron Wing, Community Health Sheffield

Publication of this book was aided by the generous support of the Kingshill Research Centre, Victoria Hospital, Swindon.

# Introduction

## Background: mental health services for the elderly

The mental health problems and needs of older people are similar to those of other groups, with the exception of age-specific illnesses, primarily dementia. As with other adult groups, depression, alcoholism and psychoses are prevalent among older people. As the number of people aged 65 years and over increases, the pressure on mental health services for the elderly will, inevitably, increase. This is compounded by the fact that older people are more likely have coexisting physical problems, particularly those associated with old age (heart disease, osteoporosis, arthritis, etc.). Carers of older people with mental health problems may also be older themselves (Department of Health (DoH), 1997) and this means that they may need more assistance from mental health and social services.

The prevalence of depression in people over 65 years old in the UK is 15% in the general community, 25% in general practice patients and around 30% in residential homes. For dementia, these figures have been put at 5% in the community and approximately 80% in residential and nursing homes. It is estimated that 20% of people aged 80 suffer from dementia (North of England Evidence Based Guideline Development Project, 1997) and 80% of these are cared for in the community. Thirty per cent of elderly people admitted to hospital suffer from delirium (Macdonald, 1997).

## Background: clinical audit

In recent years, clinical audit has become an important part of all health services. The DoH Working Paper *Medical Audit* (DoH, 1990) outlined the requirement for all doctors to participate in audit, and throughout the 1990s this expectation expanded to include clinicians of all professions. The importance of clinical audit is highlighted in the recent White Paper *The New NHS: modern, dependable* and will gain increasing importance as clinical governance is implemented.

Clinical audit is a useful and practical method of ascertaining whether services provided are effective, efficient and of a high quality. It is used to review practice by systematically monitoring whether clinical care meets pre-agreed standards.

As this book will demonstrate, many aspects of care and treatment (from admission to discharge and beyond) are amenable to clinical audit. Clinical audit should not be a difficult or daunting prospect – small projects focusing on narrow areas of practice are often as worthwhile as more complex ones. Clinical audit should be a multi-disciplinary activity, with all staff whose practice is included in that audit being involved from the beginning.

There are several points which are crucial to carrying out successful audit:

- careful planning;
- asking clear questions;
- setting clear and measurable standards;
- attempting to set standards on the basis of evidence;
- taking a multi-disciplinary approach;
- if questionnaires are to be used, ensuring the responses can be clearly interpreted and analysed;
- being clear about methods of analysis when planning a project; and
- avoiding complicated projects – simple ones usually achieve the most and are easiest to carry out.

## The aim of the book

This book is intended to support people working in mental health services for the elderly who are undertaking, or planning to undertake, clinical audit projects, by:

- providing ideas for project topics;
- providing ideas for project methods;
- providing examples of standards from other services that they can use locally;
- facilitating benchmarking against other services' standards; and
- providing contact details of others who have undertaken clinical audit projects in mental health services for the elderly.

The book contains 42 clinical audit projects, all of which have been carried out in practice (with some still in progress). The projects have been divided into topic areas and formatted into structured abstracts for ease of use.

It is hoped that the information about the clinical audit projects included is sufficient to help anyone undertaking an audit to begin to design their own project.

All the projects were submitted either by the clinical audit lead or by the clinical audit department. Queries about any of the individual projects must be directed to the person named at the end of the project example. We were overwhelmed by the enthusiasm and support of these individuals and groups. We hope that readers will be inspired by the great range of projects.

## Themes arising from the projects

There were some useful points raised by the contributors that should be borne in mind when planning a clinical audit. Several people highlighted the need to involve all relevant disciplines and agencies as early as possible in the audit cycle (Fig. 1). It was felt by some contributors that involving staff early in the project and agreeing standards and methods with all staff can help gain cooperation and involvement and predispose people to changing (and thereby improving) clinical practice.

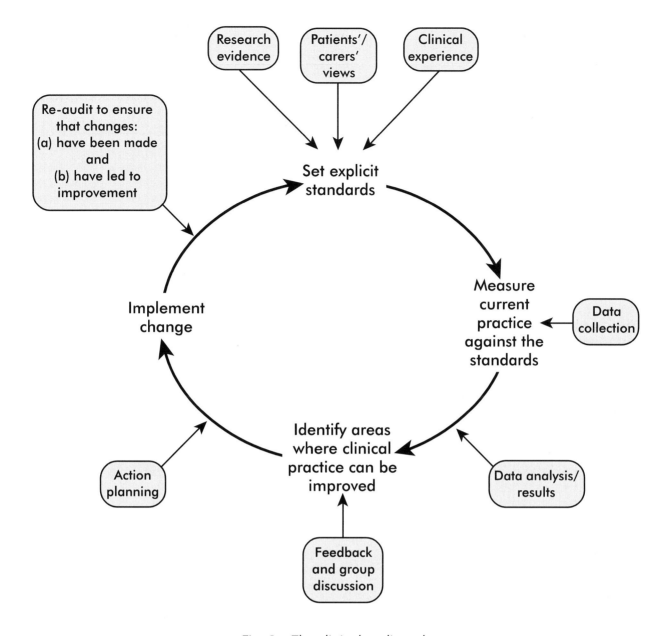

*Fig. 1    The clinical audit cycle*

The importance of ensuring the usefulness of both the standards and the audit itself was noted by several people. In a few cases, the standards that were used could not be measured as the necessary information was not available in the patients' notes. In order to avoid wasting time, it is important to consider, before beginning the audit, what information can be accessed.

# Key to reading the clinical audit project reports

Background | Why the audit was considered important.

Aim | The aims and objectives of the project.

Standards | Measurable standards against which practice was compared.

Evidence | Evidence on which the standards were based.

Staff involved | The staff involved in the clinical audit project.

Sample | The patients, clients, etc. involved in the project.

Data collection | How the data were collected.

Data analysis | What type of analysis the data were subjected to.

Key findings | Findings relating to the standards.

Feedback | Who the findings were fed back to and in what form.

Change | Suggestions for changes in practice arising from the findings. Also any significant things which either helped or prevented change from being implemented.

Re-audit | Plans for re-audit.

Resources | The amount of staff time taken to complete the audit cycle and other costs or resources needed.

Notes | Problems encountered in undertaking the clinical audit project, aspects that the contributors would change if repeating the project and advice for anyone attempting to conduct a similar audit.

Contact | Details of the person to whom further enquiries about the specific project example should be directed.

Shading draws attention to stages of the clinical audit cycle which are crucial and which are often omitted.

This book contains example of 'real-life' clinical audit projects. The projects are examples of the range of audit topics and methods undertaken in mental health services for older people, and the information has been willingly volunteered by people working within these services. Some of the examples do not contain information under all the above headings.

The projects in this book are not intended to be recommended gold standard audit projects.

**Important note**

The projects described in this book have been submitted to the Royal College of Psychiatrists' Research Unit by mental health service staff. Inclusion in this book does not indicate endorsement by the Research Unit, and the College takes no responsibility for the quality of the projects reported herein. All questions concerning specific projects should be directed to the submitting trust.

# The clinical audit projects

# Acceptance criteria to mental health services for older people

| | |
|---|---|
| Background | There was believed to be an inconsistent approach. Written acceptance criteria had been developed in only one locality. If the wrong patients are accepted, the clinical skills available may not meet their needs. |
| Aim | To improve clinical processes, organisational processes and use of resources. |
| Standards | Different standards were agreed for each of the various elements of the service, for example, day hospital, community mental health trust, in-patient department, including: |

1 Client will not be accepted to the community mental health services if either of the exclusions apply:
- client's physical illness or disability requires primary intervention; or
- client's needs will be more appropriately met by other specialist services.

2 Client must meet all of the following:
- client must have a mental health problem;
- client must reside in the locality in which his/her service is based, i.e. in the locality, or outside the locality but still registered with the relevant practice;
- client must be 70+ unless exhibiting signs of early-onset dementia;
- consent of the general practitioner is obtained by the referring agent; and
- review dates will be set every 4 weeks and documented in the notes.

| | |
|---|---|
| Evidence | Policy was in place which was revisited/amended and taken on board by all localities. It was tailored to need. |
| Staff involved | Multi-disciplinary teams from all three localities. Original meetings combined for joint planning. |
| Sample | Not recorded. |
| Data collection | Patient notes. |
| Key findings | Audit still in progress. |
| Change | Audit still in progress. |
| Notes | Pilots and data collection in progress. It is a big venture, with 10 individual audits. |
| Contact | Wendy Searle, Clinical Audit Manager, Severn NHS Trust, Rikenel, Montpellier, Gloucester GL1 1LY. Tel: 01452 901073; Fax: 01452 891158; Email: caudit@clinaudit.demon.co.uk. |

# General practitioner referrals

| | |
|---|---|
| Background | Opportunity to evaluate a service to be re-provided and reconfigured. |
| Aims | • To improve clinical processes, organisational processes, health outcomes, user/carer satisfaction and use of resources.<br>• To evaluate the effectiveness of a managed-care process model of community mental health services for older adults. |
| Standards | 1 All cases will be allocated within 1 working day of receipt of referral.<br>2 Initial contact will be made with all patients within 2 working days of referral.<br>3 The referral will be acknowledged within 3 working days.<br>4 Assessment will start within 5 working days of referral.<br>5 Initial screening assessment will be completed within 12 working days of referral.<br>6 A screening assessment review meeting will take place within 15 working days of referral (i.e. within 3 working days of the completion of the assessment).<br>7 The referring general pracitioner will be notified of the outcome of the review meeting within 20 working days of referral (i.e. within 5 working days of the review meeting having taken place). |
| Evidence | Local consensus and research evidence. |
| Staff involved | Clinicians to access data and some to extract and interpret data. |
| Sample | Consecutive referrals to the service. |
| Data collection | MHC II database. |
| Key findings | • 92.9% of cases were allocated on the day of referral.<br>• 90.6% of patients began their assessments within 5 days of referral, with a median of 2 days.<br>• 95.2% of screening assessments were completed within 12 days of referral, with a median of 2 days.<br>• 97.1% of screening assessment reviews took place within 15 days of referral.<br>• 97.2% of screening assessment outcomes were reported back to the referring general practitioner within 15 days of referral.<br>• The typical experience of referral and screening assessment is that the process of assessment is completed within 5 days of a referral being received.<br>• Over 4 years, referrals increased by 72%, but acute admissions increased by just 10%. This is a significant reduction in the propensity to admit from 29% to 15%.<br>• There was no information available for standards 2 and 3. |
| Feedback | Within the trust, to health authority purchasers and in professional press. |
| Change | None recommended. |
| Re-audit | Rolling programme. |

| | |
|---|---|
| Resources used | No reliable estimates. |
| Notes | Pressure on clinical time. Without computer data systems such an audit is not possible. There needs to be clinical ownership to ensure cooperation. |
| Contact | Dr Graham Stokes, The David Parry Suite, St Michael's Hospital, Premier Health NHS Trust, Trent Valley Road, Lichfield, Staffordshire WS13 6EF. Tel: 01543 442 010 or 01543 414 555; Fax: 01543 416 715. |

# Referrals to community psychiatric nurses

| | |
|---|---|
| Background | It was felt that some patients were being referred inappropriately and should be referred to a psychiatrist rather than a community psychiatric nurse (CPN). |
| Aims | • To improve clinical and organisational processes.<br>• To determine the number of inappropriate referrals.<br>• To determine the adequacy of information given at referral. |
| Standards | 1 Patients must meet referral criteria.<br>2 Information given must meet minimum standards. |
| Evidence | Local consensus. |
| Staff involved | CPNs, psychiatrists. |
| Sample | Six months' referrals gave a sample of 266. |
| Data collection | CPNs completed a data collection form for each referral and returned it to clinical audit department. |
| Data analysis | Data were analysed using the Borland Paradox Relational Database. |
| Key findings | • 93% were appropriate referrals but information given at referral was poor.<br>• Less than 40% gave basic information (e.g. carer's name)<br>• Only 14% gave full clinical information. |
| Feedback | Report was circulated to, and discussed by, the multi-disciplinary audit group. Presentation to general practitioners was discussed but decided against. |
| Change | Production of a separate CPN referral letter for general practitioners was considered, but it was decided that it would be difficult to gain their cooperation. A form for taking telephone referrals was introduced to ensure secretaries get full information in the absence of a CPN. |
| Re-audit | No plans. |
| Resources used | Audit staff time: 25 hours. |
| Notes | CPNs were reluctant to consider any referrals inappropriate. |
| Contact | Sylvia Warwick, Clinical Audit and Research Manager, Fair Mile Hospital, Wallingford, Oxon OX10 9HH. Tel: 01491 651 281; Fax: 01491 651 128. |

*Clinical audit in mental health services for elderly people*

# Time taken to respond to a referral

| | |
|---|---|
| Background | The team thought that it was responsive to clients', carers' and referrers' needs and wished to check that this was so. |
| Aim | To ensure the service was responsive to clients', carers' and referrers' needs. |
| Standards | 1 Response time for each referral will be within the period requested by the referrer.<br>2 All clients referred will be seen within 2 weeks.<br>3 Urgency must be recorded by the person taking the referral. |
| Evidence | The first standard is based on common sense. The second standard was decided upon as a result of team discussion, using past practice as a basis for the decision. The third standard concerns administrative practice. |
| Staff involved | Secretarial staff record the urgency of a referral when it is made and, in the case of referrals received by letter, check the urgency of the referral. The consultant clinical psychologist summarises the data. |
| Sample | 364 referrals. |
| Data collection | From database. |
| Key findings | • 96.7% of urgent referrals were seen within 24 hours.<br>• 91% of referrals requiring a 2–3-day response were seen within the time requested.<br>• 100% of non-urgent referrals (where this was recorded) were seen within 2 weeks.<br>• 95.1% of referrals where no 'urgency' was recorded were seen within 2 weeks.<br>• 99.5% of all clients assessed were seen within 2 weeks. |
| Feedback | Multi-disciplinary team: psychiatrists, CPNs, clinical psychologists, occupational therapists. |
| Change | Monitoring of urgency and date of first appointment is routine and will be maintained. |
| Re-audit | Unknown. |
| Contact | Sara Turner, Psychology Department, South West London and St George's Mental Health NHS Trust, Springfield University Hospital, 61 Glenburnie Road, London SW17 7DJ. Tel: 020 8682 6249; Fax: 020 8682 6256. |

# Alcohol histories in medical notes in psychiatric wards for the elderly

| | |
|---|---|
| Background | It is generally accepted that drinking problems in older subjects are under-diagnosed. If a fuller history is taken there is evidence to suggest that more problem drinking will be discerned. |
| Aims | • To improve the diagnosis of alcohol misuse.<br>• To improve clinical processes, organisational processes and health outcomes. |
| Standards | 1 All assessments must include alcohol history.<br>2 Alcohol histories must be expressed quantitatively (i.e. in units). |
| Evidence | Research evidence (no reference provided). |
| Staff involved | Senior registrar and 2 senior house officers. |
| Sample | 55 patients – all in-patients on a specific date. |
| Data collection | Data extracted from records on to data collection form. |
| Data analysis | Data analysed manually. |
| Key findings | • 55% had no history recorded.<br>• 25% had a qualitative history.<br>• 20% had a quantitative history. |
| Feedback | Report and presentation to audit group. |
| Change | An admission pack was devised and made available on wards and in day hospitals. A teaching session by the alcohol service was commissioned. |
| Re-audit | In progress. |
| Resources used | Staff time: 30 hours. |
| Notes | The enthusiasm of junior doctors and their commitment to doing the audit and developing the admission pack meant this was one of the most efficiently run audit projects. This was a worthwhile project which can be undertaken by staff who have little time available. |
| Contact | Sylvia Warwick, Clinical Audit and Research Manager, Fair Mile Hospital, Wallingford, Oxon OX10 9HH. Tel: 01491 651 281; Fax: 01491 651 128. |

# Assessment strategy in use on an assessment ward for the elderly

| | |
|---|---|
| Background | There were concerns about the quality of assessments on the ward. A review of organic assessment in the older people's care group took place during 1997/98. The audit fed into the review. |
| Aim | To improve clinical processes. |
| Standards | 1 All clients must receive a pre-admission assessment.<br>2 All clients must receive an initial assessment.<br>3 All clients must receive a named nurse.<br>4 All clients must receive a final assessment and follow-up care. |
| Evidence | Local consensus, multi-disciplinary working party. |
| Staff involved | Nursing staff on the ward. |
| Sample | Last five clients discharged. |
| Data collection | Retrospectively. |
| Data analysis | Manually. |
| Key findings | • 80% received a pre-admission assessment.<br>• 100% received an initial assessment.<br>• Not clear if any clients had a named nurse.<br>• No documentation on final assessments. |
| Feedback | To ward staff and management and directorate research/audit leads. |
| Change | • Formal assessment process established.<br>• Pre-admission assessment by nurse and social worker.<br>• Initial and final assessment recorded in patient's notes.<br>• Staff training on record keeping.<br>• Team restructuring to improve workload management. |
| Re-audit | 6 months. |
| Resources used | Unknown. |
| Notes | Would prefer a larger sample size.<br>*Advice*: This is a simple audit to undertake if there is good record-keeping. |
| Contact | Andrew Beardsall, Clinical Audit Facilitator, Community Health Sheffield, Fulwood House, Old Fulwood Road, Sheffield S10 3TH. Tel: 0114 271 6393; Fax: 0114 271 6392. |

# Completion of information/orientation scale of the Clifton Assessment Procedures for the Elderly (CAPE) when clients are assessed

| | |
|---|---|
| Background | It is good practice for elderly clients to have a mental test score recorded on assessment. |
| Aim | To improve the clinical assessment process. |
| Standards | Completion of the information/orientation scale of the Clifton Assessment Procedures for the Elderly (CAPE; Pattie & Gilleard, 1969) for each client referred who is seen for assessment. |
| Staff involved | The team member completing the initial assessment for a first referral or re-referral is responsible for completing the scale. In practice, over 90% of assessments are currently completed by psychiatrists. Data were analysed by a consultant clinical psychologist. |
| Sample | 269 first referrals and 95 re-referrals. |
| Data collection | From database. |
| Key findings | Scores were present for 88.8% of first referrals and 69.5% of re-referrals. |
| Feedback | To team. |
| Change | The results will be discussed in a team meeting or an audit meeting to decide whether the objective should be to complete a full assessment when a client is re-referred. |
| Re-audit | Depends on decision of audit/team meeting. |
| Contact | Sara Turner, Psychology Department, South West London and St George's Mental Health NHS Trust, Springfield University Hospital, 61 Glenburnie Road, London SW17 7DJ. Tel: 020 8682 6249; Fax: 020 8682 6256. |

# Completion and implementation of a cultural needs check-list

| | |
|---|---|
| Background | The Cultural Needs Check-List (CNCL) was devised to ensure the delivery of culturally sensitive care, by facilitating the assessment of any cultural/religious needs of clients, which are then incorporated into care plans. |
| Aim | To evaluate how frequently the CNCL is completed and how far the information elicited is incorporated into care plans. |
| Standards | Patients should be asked:<br>1 about their preferred title and its pronunciation;<br>2 whether they need anything in order to practise their religion, or if there are rituals or customs of which staff would need to be aware;<br>3 whether an interpreter is needed;<br>4 whether there are any specific dietary requirements or rules/rituals associated with eating;<br>5 whether there are any rituals/routines when washing and dressing; and<br>6 whether they have any hobbies or interests. |
| Staff involved | Key workers and an assistant psychologist. |
| Sample | 22 Black and Asian users of the older adults' service. |
| Data collection | Data were collected from client files and interviews with clients. |
| Key findings | • 18% of clients' files contained completed CNCLs.<br>• 15 clients were interviewed:<br>  • 67% had not been asked about their preferred title and its pronunciation.<br>  • 87% had not been asked whether they needed anything in order to practise their religion.<br>  • 13% had not been asked whether they needed an interpreter.<br>  • 67% were not asked about specific dietary requirements.<br>  • 93% were not asked about rituals/routines when washing and dressing.<br>  • 60% were not asked about hobbies or interests.<br>• Findings related to the meeting of their needs in practice were more favourable. |
| Change | The check-list has been revised to include tick boxes to indicate that the information has been incorporated into the client's care plan. |
| Re-audit | Unknown. |
| Notes | Some clients had memory impairment which may have affected their recall of information and their capacity to remember being asked about their preferences. The fact that their needs had usually been met in practice supports this. Few clients gave specific needs relating to their culture or religion. Most were Christian and had been in England for more than 20 years. |
| Contact | Sara Turner, Psychology Department, South West London and St George's Mental Health NHS Trust, Springfield University Hospital, 61 Glenburnie Road, London SW17 7DJ. Tel: 020 8682 6249; Fax: 020 8682 6256. |

# Religion and ethnicity

| | |
|---|---|
| **Background** | When a client is admitted, each service is required to complete a computerised admission sheet. This sheet documents essential client details such as address and general practitioner, and also contains a section for recording religion. The Patients' Charter states that the National Health Service has a duty to respect clients' differing religious and cultural beliefs. |
| **Aim** | To identify whether the ethnic origin and religion of clients are being routinely documented in the nursing notes on admission to the elderly service. |
| **Standards** | 1 Presence of computerised admission sheet in the nursing notes or care plan file. <br> 2 Religion recorded on admission sheet. <br> 3 Presence of health authority elderly service record sheet in the nursing notes or care plan file. <br> 4 Ethnic group recorded on elderly service record sheet or elsewhere in the nursing notes/care plan. |
| **Evidence** | Patients' Charter standards. |
| **Staff involved** | Elderly services clinical audit group, clinical audit coordinator/assistant. |
| **Sample** | 10 clients from 7 units ($n=70$). |
| **Data collection** | Clinical audit assistant collected data from medical notes. |
| **Data analysis** | DBase, SPSS. |
| **Key findings** | • 55 admission sheets were located. <br> • 64% contained a record of the client's religion. <br> • 49% of case notes contained a record of the client's ethnic group. <br> • Ethnic group was most frequently documented on the front of the elderly service record sheet. <br> • Only one completed ethnic monitoring form could be found in the notes. <br> • Ethnic group occasionally appeared to have been confused with nationality or birthplace. <br> • Religion was generally documented on the admission sheet although provision for recording this also exists on the elderly service record sheet. |
| **Feedback** | To the clinical audit group meeting. |
| **Change** | • Consider the necessity for including a section on ethnic group on the admission sheet. <br> • Review the completion of ethnic monitoring forms and consider the necessity for retaining these forms in the care plan file. <br> • Consider including a 'tick-box' section for recording ethnic group on the elderly service record sheet. <br> • Review the completion of admission sheets to ensure that religion is being routinely recorded. |

| Re-audit | Not decided yet. |
| --- | --- |
| Resources used | Clinical audit department. |
| Notes | Significant difficulties obtaining an epidemiological sample frame. The original aim of the audit was to look at cultural or ethnic group access to elderly mental health services. This had to be simplified to secondary and not community access and also to evidential written information contained in medical notes. This topic generated much debate about whether ethnicity is self-perception or racial categories within the recognised frameworks.<br>*Advice*: Be prepared to search out the information. |
| Contact | Gina James, Clinical Quality and Audit Manager, Mental Health Services of Salford NHS Trust, Clinical Audit Department, Bury New Road, Prestwich, Manchester M25 3BL. Tel: 0161 772 3657; Fax: 0161 772 3550; Email: gjames@audit.mhss_tr.nwest.nhs.uk. |

ASSESSMENT

# Care Programme Approach

ASSESSMENT

| | |
|---|---|
| Aim | To ensure that Care Programme Approach (CPA) standards are established and in practice within the elderly services department and that the relevant information is recorded appropriately and accurately. |
| Standards | 1 Availability of a written CPA care plan within the medical/nursing notes of all clients and completion of the CPA booklet.<br>2 Named community keyworker or keyworker assigned to client.<br>3 Copies of the CPA care plan sent to the relevant people.<br>4 Social services 'patch' of client recorded. |
| Evidence | CPA care plan. |
| Staff involved | Elderly services clinical audit group, clinical audit coordinator/assistant. |
| Sample | All patients in two wards discharged or due for discharge and those registered with two units on 1 December 1995 ($n=92$). |
| Data collection | Clinical audit assistant collected data from CPA care plan booklets in nursing process files. |
| Data analysis | DBase, SPSS. |
| Key findings | • 70% of records had a CPA care plan booklet within the documentation. None contained a keyworker signature or a date, perhaps because of the design of the booklets, which do not include a space for a signature or date within the format.<br>• 97% of clients who had a CPA care plan had a named keyworker or community keyworker listed on the front page of the booklet: 22% had a named community keyworker responsible for the overall care of the client and 75% had a named keyworker.<br>• 59% of CPA care plans had the client's general practitioner (GP) listed; however, no written confirmation was found of copies being sent to the client's GP or any other people involved in the client's care. Ward staff stated that this procedure is carried out. It is also not recorded whether clients receive a copy. 23% of CPA care plans had a carer listed among the 'People involved in client's care' section. 41% of written care plans had one or more carers mentioned on page 3 of the programme (entitled 'Care plan action'), yet these carers were not listed as people involved in the client's care and therefore not listed to receive a copy of the care plan. 23% of CPA care plans had a home help listed among those involved in the client's care.<br>• Information on the social services patch was found on page 1 of the Patient Administration System registration sheet, which is usually located at the front of the medical notes. |
| Feedback | To the elderly services clinical audit group meeting. |
| Change | • Audit team to discuss the development of the design of the CPA care plan documentation, which should include a space for signature and date, and should specify both the recording of hospital keyworker and community keyworker names and of the CPA care plan booklet being sent to the client, GP and other people involved in the client's care. |

- 'People involved in the client's care' are to receive a copy of the CPA care plan booklet when this is considered appropriate.

| | |
|---|---|
| Re-audit | 8 months. |
| Resources used | Clinical audit department. |
| Notes | Problems with access to records. All records are stored in satellite units or with consultant base office.<br>*Advice*: Be prepared to search out the information. |
| Contact | Gina James, Clinical Quality and Audit Manager, Mental Health Services of Salford NHS Trust, Clinical Audit Department, Bury New Road, Prestwich, Manchester M25 3BL. Tel: 0161 772 3657; Fax: 0161 772 3550; Email: gjames@audit.mhss_tr.nwest.nhs.uk. |

# Care Programme Approach re-audit

| | |
|---|---|
| Background | Initial audit done 8 months previously. |
| Aim | To evaluate the recorded procedures contained within the Care Programe Approach (CPA) care plan booklet, in order to provide information that can lead to improvements to meet practice standards. |
| Standards | 1  Care plan booklets should have a space to insert a signature and date.<br>2  Hospital keyworker and community keyworker names should be recorded.<br>3  CPA care plan booklets should be sent to the client, general practitioner (GP) and other people involved in the patient's care and this should be noted. |
| Evidence | CPA care plan in patient notes/nursing files. |
| Staff involved | Elderly services clinical audit group, clinical audit coordinator/assistant. |
| Sample | All patients discharged between July and September 1997 ($n=25$). |
| Data collection | From CPA care plan booklets in nursing process files. |
| Data analysis | DBase, SPSS. |
| Key findings | • 80% of case notes contained a care plan booklet.<br>• 44% of booklets contained a signature and 8% contained a date of signature. A date was recorded but, because the booklet lacked a space to insert a 'date of signature', it was not clear whether it related to the 'date of signature' or the date the care plan was written.<br>• 72% of care plan booklets identified a hospital keyworker and 64% identified a community keyworker.<br>• There was evidence that 28% of care plan booklets were sent or given to the patient, 28% to the GP and 28% to others. There was no evidence that this had been done in 72% of cases. |
| Feedback | To the clinical audit group monthly meeting. |
| Change | The elderly services clinical audit group are to consider:<br>• a review of the availability of case notes when a patient is discharged;<br>• the appropriate storage of discharge files in case they are urgently required;<br>• the need for a record of the date the care plan is written;<br>• the need for a record of the date the care plan is signed;<br>• reinforcement of the standard of recording of all information sent out to people involved in a patient's welfare; and<br>• acknowledgement of the recent audit problems in constructing patient sample frames for future clinical audit developments. |
| Re-audit | Unknown. |
| Resources used | Clinical audit department. |

CARE PLANS

| Notes | Problems with access to records. All records are stored in satellite units or with consultant base office.
*Advice*: Be prepared to search out the information. |
| Contact | Gina James, Clinical Quality and Audit Manager, Mental Health Services of Salford NHS Trust, Clinical Audit Department, Bury New Road, Prestwich, Manchester M25 3BL. Tel: 0161 772 3657; Fax: 0161 772 3550; Email: gjames@audit.mhss_tr.nwest.nhs.uk. |

**CARE PLANS**

# Dates of review of care programmes

| | |
|---|---|
| **Background** | The team records the information on a database and members are sent monthly reminders of reviews due. Prompt review of care programmes was deemed to be important for keeping clinical information up to date. It is also an activity which involves most members of the teams. |
| **Aim** | To evaluate whether care programmes are reviewed on time. |
| **Standards** | All care programmes should be reviewed no later than 1 month from the review date set by the keyworker. |
| **Evidence** | Local standard decided by team discussion. |
| **Staff involved** | Keyworkers provide the information for the database on an ongoing basis, and the assistant psychologist provides monthly reminders. The consultant clinical psychologist used data on the database to calculate when reviews were done and whether the agreed standard was met. |
| **Sample** | 276 cases over one year. |
| **Data collection** | From database. |
| **Key findings** | Some clients were discharged before the care programme review date so data were presented separately for reviews and discharges. The same standard applies for discharges: the discharge must have occurred within 1 month of the care programme review due date.<br>• Care programmes reviewed on or before review date, 68%; discharges, 93% (overall 72%).<br>• Care programmes reviewed within a month of review date, 12%; discharges, 3% (overall 11%).<br>• Care programmes reviewed 1–3 months late, 14%; discharges, 4% (overall 12%) .<br>• Care programmes reviewed 3–5 months late, 4% (overall 4%).<br>• Care programmes reviewed 6–9 months late, 2% (overall 2%). |
| **Feedback** | To team. |
| **Change** | • Administrative procedures to be altered so that when a new keyworker takes over, he/she must have to inform secretary.<br>• Reminder system to be altered so that keyworkers are notified of all outstanding care programme review each month.<br>• All team members to be reminded that they should be using and reviewing care programmes when they write in team notes so that they are not totally reliant on the reminder system. |
| **Re-audit** | In 12 months, if the information is available on a new system. |
| **Contact** | Sara Turner, Psychology Department, South West London and St George's Mental Health NHS Trust, Springfield University Hospital, 61 Glenburnie Road, London SW17 7DJ. Tel: 020 8682 6249; Fax: 020 8682 6256. |

# Day hospital care plans

| | |
|---|---|
| Background | Until 1997, nurses and occupational therapists (OTs) each completed separate care plans for every client. A new format was introduced whereby staff collaborate to write a 'combined care plan'. |
| Aim | To evaluate the quality of such plans against a set of agreed standards. |
| Standards | 1 Care plan written and reviewed within 2 weeks; dated; review dates set for action points.<br>2 Agreed action reviewed on set date.<br>3 Structure of care plan: one problem per page; writing legible; black pen used; mistakes crossed through with one line, dated and initialled; and when a problem has been resolved, this should be written, dated and signed.<br>4 Content of care plan: no abbreviations, clear reference to level of nursing observation; written in language enabling delivery;relevant action specified for each problem – action descriptive of who, what and when. |
| Evidence | Not recorded. |
| Staff involved | Head occupational therapist and nurse agreed standards; assistant psychologist and honorary assistant psychologist. |
| Sample | 57 patients who had been on hospital's case-load for at least 2 weeks and were not resident on a ward. |
| Data collection | From patient files. |
| Key findings | • 84% had full plans.<br>• Of these, 31% had been written by a nurse alone, 29% by an OT alone, 35% by a nurse and OT making separate contributions and 5% by a nurse and OT jointly.<br>• Of the care plans written within 2 weeks, 40% had been completed by a nurse and 40% by an OT. 92% were dated by a nurse and 97% by an OT. 19% of actions written by a nurse and 61% of those written by an OT were reviewed on a set date.<br>• One problem was written per page by 82% of nurses and 87% of OTs. The writing was legible for 62% of nurses and 95% of OTs, and black pen was used by 100% of nurses and 97% of OTs. Mistakes were crossed through with one line by 45% of nurses and 92% of OTs, dated by 9% of nurses and 0% of OTs and initialled by 18% of nurses and 46% of OTs.<br>• When problems were resolved this was recorded by 75% of nurses and 80% of OTs, dated by 75% of nurses and 80% of OTs, and signed by 50% of nurses and 10% of OTs.<br>• Abbreviations were not used by 21% of nurses and 32% of OTs. Writing was in language enabling delivery for 95% of nurses and 100% of OTs.<br>• Relevant action was specified for each problem by 100% of nurses and OTs.<br>• Action was descriptive of 'who' for 39% of nurses and 86% of OTs, 'what' for 69% of nurses and 84% of OTs, and 'when' for 31% of nurses and 62% of OTs. |

**CARE PLANS**

| Feedback | Hospital staff |
|---|---|
| Change | Feedback will highlight areas needing improvement and recommendations made to improve practices: for example, for clients to sign care plans for evidence of an initial care plan to be kept in all cases; and for both members of staff to sign plans which have been jointly discussed to indicate that this has been done. |
| Re-audit | Yes. |
| Contact | Sara Turner, Psychology Department, South West London and St George's Mental Health NHS Trust, Springfield University Hospital, 61 Glenburnie Road, London SW17 7DJ. Tel: 020 8682 6249; Fax: 020 8682 6256. |

CARE PLANS

*Clinical audit in mental health services for elderly people*

# In-patient nursing care plans in old age psychiatry

Aim                     To ensure that the nursing care plan process is working.

Standards               1 The care plan must clearly state the name of the primary nurse and
                          all other people involved.
                        2 The primary nurse must be able to demonstrate that accountability for
                          care planning is clearly invested in an associate nurse or another
                          primary nurse in his/her absence.
                        3 The documentation must show that a clearly formulated model of
                          care is being used.
                        4 The assessment must highlight and utilise the patient's strengths as
                          well as problems.
                        5 The assessment must incorporate psychological, social and spiritual
                          as well as physical needs.
                        6 Goals must be specific, realistic and written in terms of patient's
                          behaviour.
                        7 Nursing action must be specific.
                        8 The formative evaluation must compare the patient's outcome to the
                          goal of care.
                        9 The patient must be made aware of his/her primary nurse, and then
                          the care plan is to be signed by both of them.
                        10 The care plan should be evaluated as per the evaluation date.

Staff involved          Clinical nurse manager, senior nurse manager, ward managers.

Sample                  In-patients on ward at time of data collection.

Data collection         Prospective, from patients' notes.

Key findings            Compliance with standards was as follows:
                        1 61%
                        2 100%
                        3 100%
                        4 100%
                        5 95%
                        6 100%
                        7 100%
                        8 69%
                        9 25%
                        10 68%

Change                  Care plan documentation to be reviewed to: include space for spiritual
                        need assessment; include space for primary nurse and other health care
                        professionals involved; ensure logical sequence from assessment to
                        evaluation; ensure evaluation relates to goals and objectives and ensure
                        all assessment forms are kept together in an organised way. Training
                        needs to be identified by the individual performance review and nurse
                        education coordinator.

Resources used          10 months.

Contact                 Jackie Pile, East Wiltshire Health Care NHS Trust, Clinical Development
                        Department, St Margaret's Hospital, PO Box 415, Swindon, Wiltshire
                        SN3 4GB. Tel: 01793 425006; Fax: 01793 821 906.

# Multi-disciplinary audit in two parts of the Care Programme Approach for the elderly (Part One)

| | |
|---|---|
| Aim | To ensure the Care Programme Approach (CPA) process is working. |
| Standards | 1 Response to be sent to patient/carer within 6 weeks of referral onto CPA.<br>2 All new referrals to be on a CPA and level specified within 16 weeks of the initial referral.<br>3 Care plan review to be agreed with patient and/or carer.<br>4 Review of CPA to take place within 4–6 weeks of initial meeting.<br>5 Changes at review to be identified and documented.<br>6 All patients to be seen by the consultant psychiatrist. |
| Staff involved | Team members of department of old age psychiatry. |
| Sample | All new patients referred to the service in April 1995 (n=20). |
| Data collection | From patients' notes. |
| Key findings | • 85% of patients/carers were sent a response within 6 weeks.<br>• 60% of new referrals were on a CPA but 0% had level specified within 16 weeks of initial referral.<br>• 71% of care plan reviews were agreed with patient and/or carer.<br>• 71% of reviews of the CPA took place within 4–6 weeks of the initial meeting.<br>• 92% of changes at review were identified and documented.<br>• 67% of patients were seen by the consultant psychiatrist. |
| Change | A new CPA form was designed with an area for 'CPA levels specified'. |
| Contact | Jackie Pile, East Wiltshire Health Care NHS Trust, Clinical Development Department, St Margaret's Hospital, PO Box 415, Swindon, Wiltshire SN3 4GB. Tel: 01793 425006; Fax: 01793 821 906. |

CARE PLANS

# Multi-disciplinary audit in two parts of the Care Programme Approach for the elderly (Part Two)

| | |
|---|---|
| Aim | To ensure the Care Programme Approach (CPA) process is working. |
| Standards | 1 Area of need to be identified and documented.<br>2 CPA objective(s) to be identified and documented.<br>3 Outcomes of objectives to be identified at CPA review meeting and documented.<br>4 Any resource shortfalls to be identified and documented. |
| Staff involved | Team members of the department of old age psychiatry, clinical development coordinator. |
| Sample | All new patients referred to the service in April 1995, after exceptions ($n=17$). |
| Data collection | From patients' notes. |
| Key findings | • Areas of need were identified and documented in 100% of cases.<br>• CPA objective(s) were identified and documented in 93% of cases.<br>• Outcomes of objectives were identified at CPA review meeting and documented in 64% of cases.<br>• Resource shortfalls were identified and documented in 36% of cases. |
| Change | Training in writing objectives and outcomes has taken place. The CPA form has been changed, with a change of procedure implemented to use the new form for each CPA. The corresponding screen on the information technology system has been amended. |
| Contact | Jackie Pile, East Wiltshire Health Care NHS Trust, Clinical Development Department, St Margaret's Hospital, PO Box 415, Swindon, Wiltshire SN3 4GB. Tel: 01793 425006; Fax: 01793 821 906. |

**CARE PLANS**

# User/carer involvement in care planning

| | |
|---|---|
| Aim | To identify the extent to which clients and, if necessary, clients' carers are presently involved in care planning within the elderly services. |
| Standards | All documents to contain statements about the level of user and carer involvement in the care planning process. |
| Evidence | Not recorded. |
| Staff involved | Not recorded. |
| Sample | 43 clients were randomly selected. These were divided between nine locations in the elderly services. |
| Data collection | From nursing process notes, referral letters in the medical plans, care plans and care plan notes, admission check-lists, profile documents, personal background information. |
| Data analysis | Statements describing the level of involvement in care planning were coded according to level of involvement. The data were analysed according to professional discipline, whether the statement referred to user or carer involvement, and the level of involvement. |

**Key findings**

- Evidence of user involvement was found in 48% of statements in nursing files; evidence of carer involvement was found in 21% of statements; 7% of statements did not indicate any level of user/carer involvement; and 24% did not fit into the classification system.
  - 24% of users/carers were involved at the level of informing, 23% at the level of discussing, 9% at the level of negotiation, 1% at the level of clarification and confirmation, and 12% at the level of joint planning.
- Medical statements were found for 49% of clients and these totalled 36. 6% referred to user involvement, 72% referred to carer involvement, 14% indicated no user/carer involvement and 8% did not fit into the classification system.
  - 34% of users/carers were involved at the level of informing, 36% at the level of discussing and 8% at the level of negotiation.
- 65% of clients received occupational therapy and 44 statements were found within the occupational therapy notes. 16% referred to user involvement, 36% referred to carer involvement, 36% indicated no level of user/carer involvement, and 12% did not fit into the classification system.
  - 11% of users/carers were involved at the level of informing, 39% at the level of discussing, and 2% were involved at the level of negotiation.
- 35% of clients received physiotherapy and 22 statements were found in the physiotherapy records. 9% referred to user involvement, 59% indicated no level of user/carer involvement, and 32% did not fit into the classification system.
  - 4.5% were involved at the level of informing and 4.5% were involved at the level of discussing.

CARE PLANS

| Change | • Systems for involving users/carers in care planning to be reviewed in line with the following standards: |
|---|---|

Change

• Systems for involving users/carers in care planning to be reviewed in line with the following standards:
  • initial consultation assessment to be discussed and explained with user and/or carer and documented in response to general practitioner referral;
  • admission care plan to be formulated on the day of admission by admitting nurse or nominated deputy in consultation with user and/or carer;
  • in-depth assessment must be completed within two weeks of admission.
• Guidelines to be developed in the use of the classification scale if it is to be incorporated into clinical practice.
• Systems for recording care planning to be reviewed.

Contact

Gina James, Clinical Quality and Audit Manager, Mental Health Services of Salford NHS Trust, Clinical Audit Department, Bury New Road, Prestwich, Manchester M25 3BL. Tel: 0161 772 3657; Fax: 0161 772 3550; Email: gjames@audit.mhss_tr.nwest.nhs.uk.

**CARE PLANS**

# Change in prescribing practice of antidepressants (the use of an SSRI)

**Background**      Wanted to assess the use of a selective serotonin reuptake inhibitor (SSRI) (paroxetine) as a first-line treatment of depression in the elderly even though they are more expensive than older (tricyclic) antidepressants.

**Aim**
1 To improve clinical processes.
2 To assess whether SSRIs are really effective and safe (research question).

**Standards**      Against the use of tricyclic antidepressants.

**Evidence**      Research.

**Staff involved**      Psychiatrist.

**Sample**      21 patients with depression, referred by general practitioners.

**Data collection**      Interview of patients and carers.

**Key findings**      Paroxetine is an effective and safe drug in the treatment of moderate depression in the elderly.

**Feedback**      Monthly audit meeting.

**Change**      Paroxetine and probably other SSRIs could be used as a first-line treatment of depression in the elderly.

**Re-audit**      Unknown.

**Resources used**      8 hours.

**Notes**      More research than clinical audit.

**Contact**      Dr R. Fieldsend, Clinical Audit Lead, Chiltern Community Mental Health Team, Rectory Meadow Surgery, School Lane, Old Amersham, Bucks HP7 0HG. Tel: 01494 724422; Fax: 01494 724117.

# Antipsychotic drugs in continuing care

**Background**

Limited research literature suggests the antipsychotic effect of neuroleptic drugs has a role in reducing behavioural problems associated with dementia. There is no evidence to support the view that non-specific sedation is effective in controlling these problems.

**Aims**

1 To improve clinical processes and use of resources.
2 To assess whether prescription was rational and logical and to ensure that drugs were not overused and were stopped when appropriate.

**Standards**

1 Having at least three symptoms from a tetrad of diurnal restlessness, active aggression, irritability and agitation (or at least one of these symptoms to a severe degree) would be the indication for prescribing antipsychotics.
2 90% of those on regular antipsychotics should be on ≤100 mg thioridazine equivalent per day.
3 Those patients with the most severe problems could be expected to have had their medication reviewed most recently.
4 Patients must not remain on the same dose of antipsychotic for more than a year without formal review.
5 Patients who require physical help with all aspects of daily living must not be on antipsychotic drugs.
6 Patients rated as having depressed mood of at least moderate severity would be reviewed in more detail for possible trial of antidepressants.

**Evidence**

Research evidence refined through original audit.

**Staff involved**

Nursing staff in old age wards and consultant psychiatrist.

**Sample**

38 patients on regular antipsychotics and 46 patients receiving no psychotropic medication, followed up from previous audit. In the second audit, 29 patients formed the new regular antipsychotics group and 49 formed the new no psychotropic medication group.

**Data collection**

From medication card file with assessment of activity of daily living function and both frequency and severity of 12 behavioural problems.

**Data analysis**

$t$-test, $U$-test and chi-squared.

**Key findings**

- Of the 38 originally receiving regular antipsychotics, 17 had died (44.7%), 11 were on no medication (28.9%), one was receiving night sedation only (2.6%), two were receiving discretionary antipsychotics only (5.2%), and seven patients were still alive and on regular antipsychotics (18.4%).
- Of the 46 patients receiving no psychotropic medication in the original study, 22 were dead (47.8%), two were receiving regular antipsychotics (4.3%), one had been discharged (2.2%), and 21 were still alive and receiving no psychotropic medication (45.6%).
- In the second audit, 58.7% required physical assistance with walking, 50% with feeding, 75% with transfer from bed to chair, 91.3% with toileting and 98% with dressing. 82% were incontinent of urine and 77% incontinent of faeces more than once a week. Patients in the

regular antipsychotic group were less dependent but no different in age.

- In the second audit, 44.8% of the regular antipsychotic group were on a high-potency preparation and 20.7% also received a regular hypnotic. The median thioridazine equivalent dose per day was 30 mg (range 7–150 mg). Two patients were receiving carbamazepine in anticonvulsant dosage based on reports of its use in controlling behaviour disturbance associated with dementia. 23 of the remaining 27 patients in the regular antipsychotic group were on ≤ 100 mg thioridazine equivalent per day (82.5%), 11 of whom were on 25 mg per day.
- Among those receiving regular antipsychotics, 18 patients had three or four core problems (or at least one to a severe degree), nine had one or two core problems, and two patients had no core problems. 10 patients in the no psychotropic medication group were in the most severe category, 18 in the middle category, and 21 had no core problems. Thus, 72% of patients were correctly categorised for antipsychotic prescription.
- The regular antipsychotic group presented more behavioural problems. Those with the most severe problems had been prescribed high-potency drugs. The severity of core behavioural problems (i.e. diurnal restlessness, aggression, irritability and agitation) remained more severe on high-potency drugs.
- At the end of the second audit, 93.6% of patients were felt to be on appropriate antipsychotic regimes, including those on no medication.

| | |
|---|---|
| Feedback | Local feedback and international publication. Several local and national (Scotland) presentations. |
| Change | From the second audit, 1 patient had antipsychotic medication discontinued, and 9 had their medication changed. |
| Re-audit | In progress. |
| Resources used | Nurses: 5–10 minutes per patient, per rating, per study. Psychiatrist: 50–60 hours. |
| Notes | Standardisation of nurses' ratings across wards before each audit.<br>No problems with access.<br>Spot check methodology prevented errors in data collection over time.<br>*Advice*: preparation, preparation and preparation. Ensure definitions are accurate, ratings standardised and time set aside. |
| Contact | Peter J. Connelly, Consultant Psychiatrist, Murray Royal Hospital, Muirhall Road, Perth PH2 7BH. Tel: 01738 621 151; Fax: 01738 440 431.<br>record of relevant information. |

# Early detection of antipsychotic side-effects

| | |
|---|---|
| Background | Side-effects were often missed, and this led leading to non-compliance and suffering. |
| Aim | To train non-medical staff to examine for akathisia, extrapyramidal side-effects and tardive dyskinesia. |
| Standards | 50% of eligible patients to be screened within six months. |
| Evidence | USA guidelines (American Psychiatric Association, 1997), CSAG (Clinical Standards Advisory Group) report (CSAG, 1995), service user involved in standard setting. |
| Staff involved | Psychiatrists, research assistant, service manager, user representative. |
| Sample | 382 patients selected by keyworkers. |
| Data collection | Data collected on standardised form filled in by keyworkers. |
| Data analysis | Analysed on SPSS. |
| Key findings | • Detection of side-effects can be improved.<br>• Non-medical staff can be trained to screen.<br>• No adverse clinical effects. |
| Feedback | To trust board. |
| Change | • Need a regular post to supervise/train staff.<br>• Annual structured screening for akathisia, extrapyramidal side-effects and tardive dyskinesia is advised.<br>• Further reduction is needed in the management of these conditions. |
| Re-audit | Not yet planned. |
| Resources used | One full-time research assistant, half a session a week of a consultant psychiatrist's time, £25,000 grant from regional health authority. |
| Notes | Get sound backing from consultant body. Helped by sympathetic management and a good research assistant. Hindered by reluctance of some staff to do assessments. |
| Contact | Robert Chaplin, Tooting and Furzedown CMHT, Springfield Hospital, London SW17 7DJ. Tel: 020 8682 6439. |

**MEDICATION**

# Use of neuroleptic medication – dementia unit

MEDICATION

| | |
|---|---|
| Background | Overall investigation of neuroleptic use. |
| Aims | 1 To improve clinical processes.<br>2 To determine whether pre-agreed standards for prescribing of neuroleptics for elderly patients with dementia were met.<br>3 To survey the prescribing practice of individual consultants in old age psychiatry. |
| Standards | 1 40% of patients should not be on neuroleptics at discharge.<br>2 Of those patients on neuroleptics, 100% should be on only one at discharge (those on more than one should have a reason why stated in the notes).<br>3 No patients on neuroleptics should be on an anticholinergic for treatment of extrapyramidal side-effects.<br>4 No patients on neuroleptics should be on another drug of a chemically related structure.<br>5 Less than 5% of patients on neuroleptics should be treated via depot administration at discharge.<br>6 Where neuroleptics are prescribed 'as required', the drug card file should specify the time interval between doses or maximum daily dose. |
| Evidence | Local consensus and *British National Formulary*. |
| Staff involved | Pharmacists, consultant psychiatrists, audit staff. |
| Sample | Four consultant teams involved. Last 30 patients discharged by each team from unit during August/September 1997. If the patient had a repeat or respite admission only the most recent admission was included. |
| Data collection | Case notes and drug card files. |
| Data analysis | Data recorded on pro formas were analysed by audit staff using EPI6 software and a report was produced. |
| Key findings | • Overall findings satisfactory: 4 of 6 standards met by all consultant teams.<br>• The proportion of patients on neuroleptics was similar across all consultant teams.<br>• The documentation of 'as required' medication was unsatisfactory for one consultant team.<br>• Consultant teams prescribed neuroleptics in low doses and roughly equal proportions of typical/atypical neuroleptics. |
| Feedback | To consultant teams involved, presented to all medical staff at audit meeting, and included in trust's annual audit report. |
| Change | Considerable discussion of the most suitable drug for use in dementia. One team required increased emphasis on proper documentation of 'as required' prescriptions. |
| Re-audit | No definite time set yet. |

*Clinical audit in mental health services for elderly people*

| Resources used | 3 days for audit staff, 2 days for pharmacy staff, and 3 hours for meetings. |
| --- | --- |
| Notes | A straightforward audit providing valuable information. |
| Contact | Mrs Ruth McDonald, Homefirst Community Trust, Audit Department, Spruce House, Braid Valley Site, Cushendall Road, Ballymena, County Antrim BT43 6HL. Tel: 01266 635 292; Fax: 01266 44 221. |

**MEDICATION**

# Laxative use in a dementia unit

| | |
|---|---|
| Background | An investigation of the management of constipation in elderly people with dementia. |
| Aim | To determine whether pre-agreed standards for prescribing of laxatives for elderly patients with dementia were met. |
| Standards | 1 There will not be more than 50% of patients on laxatives.<br>2 Of those on laxatives, 70% or more will be on a single laxative.<br>3 Of those on 2 or more laxatives, 100% will be on laxatives with different modes of action.<br>4 Less than 10% of patients will have received sodium picosulphate.<br>5 Less than 30% of patients will have received co-danthramer. |
| Staff involved | Pharmacists, consultant psychiatrists, clinical audit staff. |
| Sample | For each consultant team admitting to the unit, the last 30 patients discharged in 1996 or all patients discharged in 1996 (whichever greater). If the patient had a repeat or respite admission, only the most recent admission was included. |
| Data collection | Case notes and drug card files. |
| Data analysis | Data recorded on pro formas were analysed by audit staff using EPI6 and a report was produced. |
| Key findings | • Wide variation between consultant teams in the number of patients on laxatives. Most patients were on only one laxative. All patients on more than one laxative were on drugs with different modes of action.<br>• Osmotic laxatives were most commonly used, followed by stimulant laxatives, followed by bulk-forming laxatives.<br>• Less than 30% of patients on laxatives were on co-danthramer. |
| Feedback | To consultant teams involved, presented to all medical staff at an audit meeting, presented at the Northern Ireland-Wide Audit Conference and included in annual audit report. |
| Change | • A policy was developed for laxative use in the unit.<br>• Consultant teams to ensure that junior medical and nursing staff are educated about laxative use.<br>• Dietician asked to provide dietary analysis of fibre intake for patients in the unit. |
| Re-audit | After 2 years. |
| Resources used | 15 hours of audit staff time, 15 hours of pharmacists' time, 4 hours of meetings. |
| Notes | A straightforward audit that provides valuable information. |
| Contact | Mrs Ruth McDonald, Homefirst Community Trust, Audit Department, Spruce House, Braid Valley Site, Cushendall Road, Ballymena, County Antrim BT43 6HL. Tel: 01266 635 292; Fax: 01266 44 221. |

MEDICATION

# Assessing the usefulness of brain scanning in the diagnosis of dementia

| | |
|---|---|
| Aims | To establish whether request forms for computerised tomography (CT) brain scans and report forms were completed in such a way as to maximise the clinical value of undertaking this investigation. |
| Standards | 1 Standard set for CT request forms.<br>2 Standard set for CT report forms. |
| Evidence | Local consensus and research evidence. |
| Staff involved | Consultant psychiatrist, trainee psychiatrist, consultant radiologists, clinical audit staff. |
| Sample | Selected from information obtained on requests and reports over 12 months ($n=69$). |
| Data collection | From CT request forms and reports. |
| Data analysis | Frequency count. |
| Key findings | • 41% of report and request forms available for audit.<br>• Weaknesses in request and report forms identified.<br>• Need to improve both established. |
| Feedback | To departments of old age psychiatry and radiology, and to clinical audit department. |
| Change | Implementation of new information on request forms and new pro forma on reporting, amounting to a 'dementia protocol' agreed by old age psychiatry and radiology departments. |
| Re-audit | 1 year. |
| Resources used | Audit cycle not yet completed. Took 1–2 weeks in total. |
| Contact | Dr R. I. Tobiansky, Silkstream Unit, Colindale Hospital, Colindale Avenue, London NW9 5HG. Tel: 020 8200 1555; Fax: 020 8205 8911. |

**CLINICAL CARE**

# Documentation of vascular risk factors in vascular dementia

Background
: Vascular dementia is the second most common form of dementia in the elderly and remains potentially treatable, or at least arrestable.

Aims
: 1 To improve clinical processes and use of resources.
2 To identify the rate of risk factors amenable to management as detected by clinical history, physical examination and investigations.

Standards
: 1 Clinical history of vascular risk factors must be recorded.
2 Physical examination must identify and record risk factors.
3 Blood screening and other investigations must be recorded.

Evidence
: Local consensus and national guidelines.

Staff involved
: Medical staff from old age psychiatry directorate and medical record officer.

Sample
: 30 patients in first phase, 10 in second (random selection of those with vascular dementia).

Data collection
: Retrospective case note study.

Data analysis
: Descriptive statistics.

Key findings
: • First phase: poor recording of historical risk factors and physical examination/investigations.
• Second phase: marked improvement in documentation.

Feedback
: Local audit committee. Audit published (Rao, 1998).

Change
: Adequate attention must be paid to vascular risk factors and recording. Appropriate investigations should be carried out: computerised tomography scan cannot be relied on.

Re-audit
: Late 1998.

Resources used
: 30 hours (1 clinician) – planning, data analysis and collection, dissemination.

Notes
: Think carefully about the potential usefulness and validity of such a project.

Contact
: Dr Michael Philpot, Old Age Psychiatry Directorate, Maudsley Hospital, Denmark Hill, London SE5 8AZ. Tel: 020 7919 2193; Fax: 020 7919 2506.

CLINICAL CARE

# Identification and management of constipation in a ward for the elderly mentally ill

**Background**
Constipation is common in the elderly. Factors contributing to constipation include: inadequate fluid/dietary intake, reduced mobility, physical illness, medication side-effects, laxative misuse and psychiatric illness.

**Aims**
1 To improve clinical processes.
2 To suggest basic standards/guidelines for the identification and management of constipation and modify these in the light of our findings, thus establishing practicable, generally accepted guidelines.
3 To observe and evaluate current clinical practice with regard to the assessment and treatment of constipation.
4 To assess nursing and medical staff's knowledge and awareness of constipation and its management.
5 To suggest appropriate changes and interventions to improve current clinical practice.

**Standards**
Pre-audit – none at present.

**Evidence**
There are no current formal guidelines. Standards were based on consultation with nurse ward managers, unit consultants, unit pharmacist, as well as on a literature search of management standards on geriatric medical wards.

**Staff involved**
Doctors and nurses with support from the clinical audit department and secretary.

**Sample**
Patients ($n=37$) discharged over 4 months from 3 in-patient wards (2 acute admission and 1 continuing care), all doctors ($n=8$) on wards, all regular in-patient nurses ($n=21$).

**Data collection**
Retrospectively from clinical notes (nursing and medical) using pro forma and interview of nurses and doctors using semi-structured questionnaire.

**Data analysis**
Descriptive statistics.

**Key findings**
- Constipation was common.
- Constipation was diagnosed in 23 out of the 37 cases studied.
- 6 of these 23 cases were diagnosed at the point of admission; 14 of the 23 were on pre-admission medication with constipation as a potential side-effect (such as phenothiazines, tricyclic antidepressants and opiate analgesics and antacids); 7 of the 23 were on pre-admission oral laxatives.
- 10 out of 37 had rectal examinations; 33 had abdominal palpation examinations; 19 had bowel sound examinations; 32 had hydration status examinations.
- Laxatives commonly prescribed on admission included senna (12 cases), lactulose (6 cases), phosphate enema (5 cases) and a combination of these (9 cases).
- All 8 patients on pre-admission laxatives were later found to be constipated.

- Dietary history was recorded for 15 patients.
- Clinical assessment was poor.
- Observation charts were not utilised.

| | |
|---|---|
| Feedback | Local presentation to nurses and doctors, local publication, on audit website. |
| Change | • Draft guidelines developed as a basis for more comprehensive guidelines.<br>• Complete review of current procedures and management of constipation to ensure clarity of expected standards and procedure.<br>• Establishment and implementation of unit guidelines on assessment and management of constipation based on the audit.<br>• Use of one uniform admission assessment form on all wards.<br>• Improve bowel charts.<br>(Three months allowed for all the above.)<br>• Dissemination of guidelines and education of staff on guidelines. (One month allowed.) |
| Re-audit | Mini-audits (10–15 case notes) at 2-monthly intervals for approximately 6 months. Major re-audit at 12 months. |
| Resources used | One session a week of specialist registrar time for 4–5 months. About 1 hour a week of secretarial time for this period. Some support from audit department. |
| Notes | Sample size was small owing to low turnover in our unit.<br>*Advice:* Do it over slightly longer period with more patients. |
| Contact | Dr A. K. Shah, John Connolly Unit, Ealing, Hammersmith and Fulham Mental Health NHS Trust, Uxbridge Road, Southall, Middlesex UB1 3EU. Tel: 020 8967 5045; Fax: 020 8967 5798; Email: a.k.shah@ic.ac.uk. |

**CLINICAL CARE**

# Patients found on the floor

| | |
|---|---|
| Aim | To obtain current data on incidents involving patients found on the floor in order to introduce guidelines and interventions to minimise the incidence. |
| Standards | The following information must be recorded:<br>1 position of patient found on the floor;<br>2 time and location of incident;<br>3 type of floor covering;<br>4 medical diagnosis;<br>5 relevant medications/illnesses;<br>6 number of staff on duty;<br>7 number of bank staff on duty; and<br>8 shift during which fall occurred. |
| Evidence | Local audit. |
| Staff involved | Ward manager to undertake data collection, committee of ward managers organising the audit, chaired by service manager. |
| Sample | 94 randomly selected. |
| Data collection | Retrospective data collection. |
| Data analysis | Undertaken by trust audit department. |
| Key findings | All standards were met with the exception of standard 5. It is not clear whether the relevant medications were recorded in all cases, and in one case relevant illnesses were not recorded. |
| Feedback | Via directorate of the audit group. Report produced and circulated to all relevant areas. |
| Re-audit | Yes, but no date set. |
| Resources used | Audit department, clinical time, data collection tool. |
| Contact | Gaynor Abbott, Thameside Community Healthcare NHS Trust, Level C, Mental Health Unit, Basildon Hospital, Nethermayne, Basildon, Essex SS16 5NL. Tel: 01268 593 663; Fax: 01268 598 275. |

**CLINICAL CARE**

# Resuscitation – the decision not to resuscitate

CLINICAL CARE

| | |
|---|---|
| Background | Important ethical/legal issue in old age psychiatry, particularly in relation to continuing care patients. |
| Aims | 1 To improve clinical processes and organisational processes.<br>2 To assess whether the main points of the trust policy are in effect.<br>3 To assess whether cardiopulmonary resuscitation (CPR) status is easily accessible in the notes. |
| Standards | 1 All continuing care patients should be subject to a CPR decision.<br>2 All decisions should be documented in case notes, signed and dated.<br>3 All decisions should have consultant approval.<br>4 All case notes should document discussion with relatives.<br>5 All decisions should be easily accessible in case notes. |
| Evidence | Trust policy document. |
| Staff involved | Psychiatric senior house officer gathered data, liaising with relevant ward nursing staff. |
| Sample | 67 representative acute and continuing care old age psychiatry in-patients. |
| Data collection | Case note review. |
| Data analysis | Simple calculations – no statistics. |
| Key findings | • 23 had a formal decision documented regarding CPR (or not).<br>• All of these were signed and dated (although one date had the year missing) and 21 were documented with consultant approval.<br>• 14 decisions were documented as having been discussed with relatives and in 20 the information was easily accessible in the case of an emergency.<br>• 44 did not have a CPR decision documented although in 2 instances it was documented that relatives wished to have active management including CPR (in 1 case against medical advice).<br>• Only 2 of the 23 had had their decision reviewed. |
| Feedback | To all medical staff at medical audit meeting and more detailed discussion and action plan in old age psychiatry medical business meeting. |
| Change | • All patients on the continuing care wards will be reviewed to ensure 100% implementation of the policy.<br>• Greater consideration will be given to assessing patients on acute wards for their suitability for CPR.<br>• A form to be drafted will be stapled to the inside front cover of case notes of any patient not for CPR.<br>• Trust policy will be updated to include new information. |
| Re-audit | 6 months. |

| Resources used | 3 hours for the senior house officer data gathering and preparing reports, 10 hours (30 minutes × 20 individuals) for feedback, 2 hours for redrafting policy. |
| --- | --- |
| Notes | Would be better carried out in clinical audit, rather than medical audit setting, to include nursing staff more actively in the process. |
| Contact | Dr Helen Leegood, Sussex, Weald and Downs NHS Trust, 6/7 Russell House, Bepton Road, Midhurst, West Sussex GU29 9NB. Tel: 01730 815 737; Fax: 01730 816 534. |

CLINICAL CARE

# Use of the tissue viability policy and care of pressure sores

Background

Pressure sores were a pan-Birmingham audit topic for 1997/98. The incidence of pressure sores is reported as part of the annual quality report to the purchaser. Tissue viability is a physical health issue of which registered mental health nurses may have little experience.

Aims

1 To improve clinical and organisational processes and health outcomes.
2 To see if the tissue viability policy is helping them deliver high-quality care.

Standards

1 A 'Waterlow' score must be calculated for each patient after admission.
2 Patients with a Waterlow score of 10+ must have a care plan developed to prevent pressure sores.

Evidence

Research evidence and local consensus.

Staff involved

Senior nurse, clinical audit assistant.

Sample

10 patients were selected randomly on a specified day from each of three assessment units.

Data collection

The nursing notes were looked at for evidence that the policy was being followed. An audit tool based largely on one used in the local community health trust was adopted. Further questions were asked of those patients who, at the time, had pressure sores.

Data analysis

SPSS.

Key findings

- The Waterlow score had been recorded as per the policy in 25 out of 30 cases.
- Ten patients were at risk of pressure sores.
- All 4 patients at 'high risk' had prevention plans.
- 5 out of the other 6 patients 'at risk' had a prevention plan.
- It was also found that there was insufficient appropriate seating and insufficient information available to patients and carers.

Feedback

To tissue viability group and clinical services manager.

Change

- More appropriate seating will be ordered, information about pressure sores, for patients and carers, has been provided by the National Health Service response line.
- Alternative ways for training staff about tissue viability need to be explored. The need to formulate a care plan if the Waterlow score is 10+ needs to be made explicit in the policy. This will be discussed with staff.

Re-audit

In 6–12 months.

Resources used

20 hours of senior nurse time, 20 hours of clinical audit department time.

Notes        The audit went smoothly because it used a well developed standard and
             audit tool. The clinical time needed to assess the notes was a problem.
             When re-auditing, a larger sample will be used (all clients with pressure
             sores).
             *Advice:* By looking at issues such as the information available to patients
             and carers, opportunities are opened to implement improvements, which
             can give the audit positive outcomes.

Contact      Clinical Audit Department, Mental Health Services for Older Adults,
             South Birmingham Mental Health NHS Trust, Hollyhill Unit, Rubery Lane,
             Rubery, Birmingham B45 9AY. Tel: 0121 627 8336; Fax: 0121 627
             8440.

CLINICAL CARE

# Clinical audit of modified electroconvulsive therapy

Background
- High level of prescribing of modified electroconvulsive therapy (MECT).
- Interest from clinical practitioners and MIND and the health authority.
- Previous audits undertaken by the Royal College of Psychiatrists (RCPsych) were thought to be 'top down', imposed on staff via external visits (also thought to lack indicators).

Aims
1 To improve the use of resources.
2 To ensure effective use of facilities.
3 To ensure compliance with 'best practice'.

Standards
Based on guidelines published by the RCPsych (Freeman, 1995), especially the section on the ECT suite by Dr C. Freeman and Dr J. Lambourn.

Evidence
Guidelines from the RCPsych (Freeman, 1995).

Staff involved
Consultant psychiatrist, consultant anaesthetist, MECT nursing team, clinical audit support staff.

Sample
Not applicable.

Data collection
Direct observation – quantitative data, archival data.

Data analysis
Manual, no software necessary.

Key findings
Some deficiencies in current guidelines.

Feedback
Initially to working party, subsequently to trust management and external agencies.

Change
Replacing facilities and upgrading sites.

Re-audit
Dependent on priorities.

Resources used
Approximately 100 hours.

Notes
Inaugural audit – some resistance to undertaking audit. Also some members of team would have preferred to audit 'outcome' rather than 'structure'. External agencies may have preferred research project to audit.
*Advice:* Involve management earlier in audit cycle to implement change – with approval of audit working party.

Contact
Russell Mason, Clinical Audit Office, Local Health Partnerships NHS Trust, Sampson House, St Clement's Hospital, Foxhall Road, Ipswich, Suffolk IP3 8LS. Tel: 01473 276 508; Fax: 01473 276 593.

**DEPRESSION/ DELIBERATE SELF- HARM/SUICIDE**

# Electroconvulsive therapy given to old age psychiatry service patients

Background
Electroconvulsive therapy (ECT) is a controversial but effective treatment for depression and is believed to be safe in elderly patients. Previous audit had highlighted poor documentation, poor techniques of administration, lack of a local policy and an ineffective central recording system.

Aim
To improve clinical processes and organisational processes.

Standards
1 Indications for ECT and pre-treatment investigations must be recorded.
2 Seizure duration must be monitored and re-stimulation used if it fails.
3 Pre- and post-ECT nursing check-list must be completed.
4 Outcome and reasons for termination must be recorded.
5 ECT policy must be updated (central register set up).

Evidence
National standards (Freeman, 1995).

Staff involved
Medical staff of ECT unit.

Sample
All patients over 65 years receiving ECT between July 1996 and June 1997 (n=17).

Data collection
Retrospective case note study.

Data analysis
Descriptive statistics.

Key findings
• Major improvement in documentation and technique of administration.
• Still no improvement in action over re-stimulation.
• Policy updated and central register set up.

Feedback
To hospital audit committees including user group, to health authority and summary circulated to all old age psychiatry staff.

Change
• Further development of recording documentation: new prescription and recording forms, outcome form for responsible medical officers and development, with user group, of a patient questionnaire (not specific to elderly users).
• Appointment of consultant responsible for ECT with a paid sessional commitment, honorary specialist registrar assistance and improved training as a result of the previous two points.

Re-audit
Late 1998.

Resources used
2 medical staff (consultant and senior house officer) for approximately 20 hours including planning, data collection and report writing.

Notes
Number of cases could have been greater but this was a total annual survey. Limit seizure duration criteria to one method (EEG>25 s). Much of the information used to assess outcome and adverse events is not routinely recorded. Would advise design of special report forms.

Contact
Dr Michael Philpot, Old Age Psychiatry Directorate, Maudsley Hospital, Denmark Hill, London SE5 8AZ. Tel: 020 8919 2193; Fax: 020 8919 2506.

**DEPRESSION/ DELIBERATE SELF- HARM/SUICIDE**

# The use of electroconvulsive therapy: practice, training and patients' attitudes

| | |
|---|---|
| Background | An earlier audit based on the Royal College of Psychiatrists' 1989 guidelines showed many patients did not remember verbal information given to them. |
| Aims | To improve clinical and organisational processes and user/carer satisfaction. With the publication of the *ECT Handbook* (Freeman, 1995) it was decided:<br>1 to examine the administration of ECT to elderly patients and;<br>2 to investigate patients' views of treatment. |
| Standards | Standards on concurrent medication, review, pre-medication, re-stimulation, recording, patient information, all in accordance with the *ECT Handbook*. |
| Evidence | *ECT Handbook* (Freeman, 1995). |
| Staff involved | Medical staff, ward nurses, nursing staff in ECT suite, anaesthetists, clinical psychologist. |
| Sample | All elderly patients receiving ECT over 9 months ($n=12$). |
| Data collection | Notes, prescription and medication cards, questionnaire to senior house officers (SHOs) and interviews with patients. |
| Data analysis | Data analysed manually. |
| Key findings | • Drugs which can affect seizure activity were being prescribed.<br>• Mixed and inconsistent terminology used to describe seizures.<br>• Patients could not remember being given information and nurses were not sure if leaflet was given. |
| Feedback | Elderly mental health multi-disciplinary team. All medical staff (consultants' meeting and postgraduate meeting), anaesthetists (separate trust). |
| Change | • Adopt a standardised procedure for providing information.<br>• Consider anaesthetic information leaflet.<br>• Consent interview to be recorded in notes.<br>• Consent to be obtained in non-threatening situation (i.e. not ward round).<br>• Actively elicit and record side-effects.<br>• SHO training to include Hamilton cuff and correct timing of seizures.<br>• Changes to elderly mental health practice backed by multi-disciplinary audit group.<br>• Revised ECT prescription card now used across whole hospital. |
| Re-audit | Re-audit of consent to treatment protocol for the elderly in 1998/99. |
| Resources used | 450 hours for interviews, data collection, analysis, report writing, dissemination, designing new ECT card, designing protocol and check-list, and staff training. |

**DEPRESSION/ DELIBERATE SELF- HARM/SUICIDE**

Notes          Anaesthetist from acute trust did not think an anaesthetics information leaflet was necessary. There were different opinions about the relevance of RCPsych guidelines to a different speciality.
*Advice*: Ensure consultant responsible for ECT training and anaesthetists are involved from the start.

Contact       Sylvia Warwick, Clinical Audit and Research Manager, Fair Mile Hospital, Wallingford, Oxon OX10 9HH. Tel: 01491 651 281; Fax: 01491 651 128.

DEPRESSION/ DELIBERATE SELF- HARM/SUICIDE

# Deliberate self-harm in patients over the age of 65 years

Background | Older adults are perceived as being at high risk of self-harm, are often depressed at the time of self-harm and can benefit from treatment.

Aims
1 To improve clinical processes and health outcomes.
2 To establish a systematic means of identifying and effectively managing these patients.

Standards
1 All adults over 65 years presenting with deliberate self-harm must be referred to a specialist service.
2 All referred patients must be seen within one day of referral.
3 All referred patients must be reviewed by senior staff within 5 working days.
4 All patients must have a statement of diagnosis.
5 All patients must be followed up.

Evidence | Based on national guidelines – *The General Hospital Management of Adult Deliberate Self-Harm* (Royal College of Psychiatrists, 1994).

Staff involved | Audit coordinator, consultant psychiatrist.

Sample | 34 patients.

Data collection | Case note review.

Key findings
• Most referred patients are seen quickly (75%).
• Most are reviewed by senior staff (80%).
• All patients have a diagnosis (100%).

Feedback | Mental health directorate, clinical audit meeting.

Change | Well-defined anticipated pathway of care, primary care education, joint medical/nursing assessment, review by senior staff is ensured. Audit confirmed that the trust population is relatively well-circumscribed.

Re-audit | 12 months.

Resources used | Audit coordinator, 8 hours; writing presentation, 3 hours.

Notes | Potential breaches of patient confidentiality if patients are identified as being 'not referred'. Better data collection form (being written). Ideal topic – 'do-able' and rewarding.

Contact | Dr Robert Colgate, Bro Morgannwg NHS Trust, Glanrhyd Hospital, Tondu Road, Bridgend CF31 4LN. Tel: 01656 752 752; Fax: 01656 753 883.

# Suicides in the community

| | |
|---|---|
| Background | In 1992 the Royal College of Psychiatrists' Section of Old Age Psychiatry asked each region to collect data on elderly suicides and non-accidental deaths. In Wessex the findings revealed the great majority were not known to specialist services. In those that were there was a poor rate of suicide assessment. |
| Aims | • To improve clinical processes and health outcomes.<br>• To assess how well the specialist service identified risk of suicide in newly referred patients with depression, the treatment and communication with general practitioners (GPs). |
| Standards | 1 All patients should have risk assessment when first seen.<br>2 All patients with functional illness should be assessed for risk of suicide.<br>3 All patients should have a formulation and treatment programme communicated to the GP.<br>4 An alcohol history should be obtained from all patients. |
| Evidence | Consensus of medical staff in service. |
| Staff involved | All medical staff making assessments. |
| Sample | 1 month of referrals. |
| Data collection | Retrospectively by measuring assessment form against audit criteria. |
| Key findings | • Low level of assessment of suicide risk.<br>• Moderate level of assessment of alcohol history.<br>• Good standard of formulation and treatment programme. |
| Feedback | Medical staff in service. |
| Change | Altering the assessment pro forma to include specific questions on past suicide attempt and assessment of risk. |
| Re-audit | 6 months. |
| Resources used | 12 hours. |
| Notes | This is part of a review of elderly community suicides. All cases of suicide occurring in the community are audited with their GP every 1–2 years to identify practice issues needing improvement. |
| Contact | Henry Rosenvinge, Southampton Community Health Services NHS Trust, Thornhill Unit, Moorgreen Hospital, Botley Road, West End, Southampton SO30 3JB. Tel: 01703 475 242; Fax: 01703 465 014. |

**DEPRESSION/ DELIBERATE SELF- HARM/SUICIDE**

# Day hospital standards

**Background**    New day hospital recently opened with new set of objectives and recently set standards.

**Aim**    To check that standards address areas needing improvement.

**Standards**

1 All referrals to be made on the day hospital referral form and the aims of attendance to be clearly stated.
2 A keyworker must be assigned to every patient and this must be documented in the patient's notes.
3 Within 2 weeks of the referral being received a short standard letter will be sent to the general practitioner (GP) to inform him or her of the patient's referral to the day hospital.
4 Within 8 weeks of the first attendance a multi-disciplinary team review must be held and a treatment plan formed. This should be recorded on the review form, which should be placed in the patient's notes. After this review, a further letter to the GP should be sent outlining the treatment plan.
5 For all new patients in their first 8 weeks of attendance:
   • A standard assessment form must be completed for every patient which notes physical examinations and investigations unless these have already been done on the ward. The whole assessment form should be completed within the first 2 weeks.
   • The keyworker must make an entry in the notes at least once a week.
   • The doctor must make an entry in the notes at least once a week and include comments on mental state.
6 From 8 weeks onwards:
   • The keyworker must make an entry in the notes at least once a month.
   • The doctor must make an entry in the notes at least once a month which includes details of mental state examination.
7 Multi-disciplinary reviews are to be held at 8-week intervals for all patients.
8 All groups attended must be documented for each patient by the group facilitator.
9 A full discharge summary must be sent to the GP within one week of final discharge and a copy of this summary placed in the notes.

**Evidence**    Local consensus.

**Staff involved**    Senior house officer in psychiatry, all day hospital staff.

**Sample**    All patients attending the day hospital (n=30).

**Data collection**    By senior house officer from case notes.

**Key findings**    Documentation was not meeting set standards, particularly in relation to junior doctor assessments and letters to GPs.

**Feedback**    To all day hospital staff and all junior doctors.

ORGANISATIONAL/ MANAGEMENT PROCESSES

| Change | Some objectives too ambitious but doctor documentation must be improved (new doctor appointed). Medical staffing levels must be improved, e.g. some months there are no junior doctors in post. |
|---|---|
| Re-audit | 1 year. |
| Resources used | 30 hours. |
| Notes | Some suspicion on the part of staff and misunderstanding of aims. Agree standards first with all staff and give advance warning of audit. |
| Contact | Dr C. Gorst-Unsworth, Consultant in Old Age Psychiatry, Worthing Priority Care NHS Trust, The Ridings, Southlands Hospital, Upper Shoreham Road, Shoreham-by-Sea, West Sussex BN43 6TQ. Tel: 01273 446 047; Fax: 01273 446 007. |

ORGANISATIONAL/
MANAGEMENT
PROCESSES

# Day hospital use and follow-up in older adults with functional mental health disorders

| | |
|---|---|
| Background | The 1995 policy change split health and social care. Pressure was brought to bear on staff to discharge earlier. There was concern about relapse levels and patient satisfaction. |

Aims

1 To measure patients' length of attendance at the day hospital.
2 To look at age, gender, physical health, psychiatric history and whether the patient lived alone, and to see whether any of these factors were related to length of attendance.
3 To measure relapse rates.
4 To look at what type of follow-up patients received.
5 To obtain patients' views on their treatment at the day hospital and their follow-up.
6 To provide feedback to staff about quality of care within the day hospital and suggest improvements where required.

Standards

None – pre-audit.
Data collected on:
1  gender
2  age
3  marital status
4  whether client lived alone
5  psychiatric history (yes/no)
6  hospital admission (yes/no)
7  electroconvulsive theory (yes/no)
8  diagnosis
9  outcome rating
10  length of attendance at day hospital (weeks)
11  relapse
12  follow-up
13  disability rating
Data were compared with those from another local day hospital.

Evidence

Research evidence (no references).

Staff involved

Clinical psychologist, psychology assistant.

Sample

56 people with functional illness referred to day hospital in 1994.

Data collection

Retrospective analysis of case notes, physical disability ratings completed by staff and semi-structured interview (administered to 31 people).

Data analysis

ANOVA (analysis of variance) of case note data. Descriptive statistics for questionnaire data.

Key findings

- 36% male, 64% female.
- Mean age 74 years, range 65–92 years.
- 14% single, 54% married, 32% widowed.
- 43% lived alone, 52% lived with spouse, 5% lived with relatives.
- 64% had a psychiatric history.
- 39% had a recent admission to an in-patient ward.

- 14% had received ECT.
- 63% had a diagnosis of depression, 29% of anxiety/depression, 2% of agitated depression, and 7% of schizoaffective illness or hallucinations.
- Approximately half the patients showed an improvement in their outcome rating.
- Length of attendance was 1–4 weeks for 14%, 5–12 weeks for 18%, 13–26 weeks for 34%, 27–52 weeks for 20%, 12–18 months for 5%, over 18 months for 5%, and 2% died during attendance.
- Relapse: 4 patients were still attending day hospital; 2 were readmitted to day hospital within 6 months; 3 were readmitted to day hospital between 6 and 12 months; 14 died; and 33 were not readmitted.
- Follow-up care was provided by community psychiatric nurses in 34% of cases, out-patient departments in 36%, physiotherapy in 5%, occupational therapy in 13%, club run by community mental health team in 7%, day centre in 13%, and respite care in 5%.
- Follow-up in less than 6 months for 23%; in 6–12 months for 27%; in 12–18 months for 13%; in over 18 months for 30%; and 7% were in contact with team until death.
- ANOVA results: trend to significance for living circumstances and psychiatric history to be associated with length of attendance.
- Of the 31 people interviewed 16% said that a leaflet about the day hospital would be useful.
- 36% of patients found all activities at the hospital were most helpful, 29% thought relaxation was, 19% the anxiety management group, 13% the quiz, 3% arts and crafts, 10% exercises, 1% physiotherapy, and 1% none.
- The least helpful activities were quiz (13%), arts and crafts (3%), relaxation (13%), exercises (3%), and none (67.7%).
- Most helpful aspects of attendance were meeting others with similar problems (80.6%), talking to staff (35.5%), going out for the day (32.3%), anxiety management group (6.5%), everything (6.5%), relaxation (3.2%), and nothing (3.2%).
- 51.6% felt they had gained a lot from attending the day hospital, 29% a little, and 19.4% no change.
- 65% were satisfied with the length of their attendance, 26% thought it was too short, one person thought it was too long and two were still attending.
- Less then half the patients felt that their discharge had been carefully planned with their views taken into account.

| | |
|---|---|
| Feedback | Audit presented at psychiatric divisional audit meeting and report circulated to all day hospital staff/managers. |
| Change | Staff are considering planning group activities and trying to take into account sensory deficits. Discharge planning is being improved. The service manager is looking at ways of providing a telephone number for clients and carers to call when needed and a carers' support group for relatives of clients with functional disorders. A regular method of obtaining clients' feedback needs to be devised. |
| Re-audit | Patient satisfaction to be measured again in early 1999. |
| Contact | (In writing) Ann Marshall, Chartered Clinical Psychologist, Newtown House, Newtown Road, Eastleigh, Hants SO50 4DB. |

ORGANISATIONAL/
MANAGEMENT
PROCESSES

# Elderly care services

| | |
|---|---|
| Background | Local audit steering group devised 16 core standards. |
| Aims | 1 To improve clinical processes, organisational processes and use of resources.<br>2 To identify to what extent these standards of care are being implemented on each elderly care ward/unit. |
| Standards | Standards were set in the following areas:<br>1 admission/discharge<br>2 care planning<br>3 use of neuroleptics<br>4 prevention and management of constipation<br>5 sleep<br>6 management of fits and seizures<br>7 prevention of pressure sores<br>8 holidays for patients<br>9 foot care<br>10 mobility<br>11 privacy and dignity<br>12 managing patients with swallowing difficulties<br>13 prevention of falls in the elderly<br>14 wheelchair safety<br>15 risk taking<br>16 creating a culturally sensitive mental health service |
| Evidence | Local consensus, trust plans, national guidelines. |
| Staff involved | Member of the clinical audit department, ward manager from ward being audited, ward manager from another site, operational manager. |
| Sample | 10 case notes randomly selected per quarter. |
| Data collection | Documentation review, site observations and staff interviews. |
| Data analysis | Excel speadsheets. |
| Key findings | • It was difficult to measure standards with time frames, as many of the assessment forms/tools were not dated.<br>• Ward managers were unaware of the need to have translation cards and cultural awareness check-lists.<br>• Training required had not yet been set up.<br>• Equipment was missing from wards. |
| Feedback | To each team for discussion and recommendations and action plans devised. Full reports were then circulated to operational managers and service directors. |
| Change | • Some of the assessment forms, tools, weight charts to be reviewed and amended to allow for date to be recorded and for more space for recordings.<br>• Review the availability of some services (dentistry, chiropody).<br>• All patients should have lockable cupboards. |

**ORGANISATIONAL/ MANAGEMENT PROCESSES**

*Clinical audit in mental health services for elderly people*

- Staff training programme to be reviewed and updated.
- All wards/units to have an up to date policy manual.
- Discussing and devising recommendations with the staff teams has helped to implement changes.
- Increased feeling of ownership.

Re-audit            12 months.

Resources used      75–100 hours.

Notes               Compiling individual reports, individual team feedback sessions and
                    action planning were very time-consuming for the audit department.
                    Because not all of the 16 standards were applicable to all areas, time
                    was wasted in some areas.
                    *Advice*: Do not audit 16 standards all in one go for all sites. Make sure
                    all relevant disciplines are involved from the start.

Contact             Paula Bramley, Clinical Audit and ICP Coordinator, Brent, Kensington,
                    Chelsea and Westminster Mental Health NHS Trust, Commonwealth
                    House, 2–4 Chalkhill Road, London W6 8DW. Tel: 020 8846 7433;
                    Fax: 020 8746 8978.

# Joint working between ward and community staff

Background
: The success of the original audit 12 months previously and the improvement in practice this generated.

Aims
: 1 To improve clinical processes, organisational processes, health outcomes, user/carer satisfaction and the use of resources.
2 Evaluation of quality of liaison between the multi-disciplinary team, ward staff and clients and carers.

Standards
: 1 The community keyworker will pass on relevant information before admission.
2 Where the client has a community keyworker, the keyworker will retain this role during and after the client's admission, with the exception of where the client is discharged to another area or where the keyworker changes during admission.
3 The community keyworker and primary nurse or their representatives will liaise weekly during the client's hospital stay.
4 The community keyworker will attend at least a ward clinical meeting at least once and then for every full month of the client's hospital stay.
5 The primary nurse will inform the community keyworker or his/her representative of any changes discussed at the ward clinical meeting if the community keyworker does not attend.
6 The community keyworker will visit the client at least once and then every full month of client's hospital stay.
7 Both the primary nurse and keyworker will attend the pre-discharge meeting to discuss the aftercare plan with client/carers/other professionals.

Evidence
: The previous year's audit on joint working and associated shortfalls identified.

Staff involved
: Nurse manager, senior staff nurse, clinical audit facilitator.

Sample
: Clients admitted to a ward over 12 months (n=24).

Data collection
: Retrospective criteria based audit of case notes.

Data analysis
: PinPoint Package – an information, collection and analysis package.

Key findings
: • The community keyworker will pass on relevant information before admission – 75%.
• Where the client has a community keyworker, the keyworker will retain this role during and after the client's admission, with the exception of where the client is discharged to another area or where the keyworker changes during admission – 100%.
• The community keyworker and primary nurse or their representatives will liaise on weekly during the client's hospital stay – 67%.
• The community keyworker will attend a ward clinical meeting at least once and then for every full month of the client's hospital stay – 95%.
• The primary nurse will inform the community keyworker or his/her representative of any changes discussed at the ward clinical meeting if the community keyworker does not attend – 83%.

**ORGANISATIONAL/ MANAGEMENT PROCESSES**

*Clinical audit in mental health services for elderly people*

- The community keyworker will visit the client at least once and then every full month of client's hospital stay – 0%.
- Both the primary nurse and keyworker will attend the pre-discharge meeting to discuss the aftercare plan with client/carers/other professionals – 86%.

| | |
|---|---|
| Feedback | To senior nurse managers and lead nurses, then by nurse manager to community mental health team and ward staff. |
| Change | • Source of information on admissions needs to be documented in the 'to come in' book.<br>• Where possible, a member of the ward team should attend the referral and feedback meetings. Where this is not possible, the minutes should be discussed at the weekly ward round.<br>• Within the progress notes, the role of each person attending should be clearly identified. Representatives from both teams should be clearly identified in the progress notes.<br>• Discussion with members of the community team to develop a format of documentation which will identify community liaison, to ensure future compliance with the relevant standard.<br>• There is a need to amend the wording of the standards to indicate that it is not essential for clients and carers who are involved in planning the clients' care and discharge to attend a formal pre-discharge meeting. |
| Re-audit | 12 months. |
| Resources used | Nurse manager, 3 days; senior staff nurse, 2 days; clinical audit facilitator, 1 day; administrator, 1 day. |
| Notes | Senior staff nurse could not get time free for final collation and report writing. If doing this again the trust would include a health care assistant and community psychiatric nurse so that the project would be owned by as many levels of staff as possible. |
| Contact | Jane Bemrose, East Yorkshire NHS Trust, Watersward, Bridlington and District Hospital, Bridlington, Yorkshire YO16 4QP. Tel: 01262 607 116; Fax: 01262 400 583. |

ORGANISATIONAL/
MANAGEMENT
PROCESSES

# Third-year medical student teaching in old age psychiatry

| | |
|---|---|
| Background | The psychogeriatric unit has a commitment to teaching, maintaining and improving standards. |
| Aims | 1 To improve user satisfaction.<br>2 To see if unit was achieving standards and identify any new areas of concern. |
| Standards | 1 Develop knowledge of clinical syndromes, principles of treatment and range of available services.<br>2 Develop skills in interview, mental state examination, present cases and assess suicide risk.<br>3 See a wide range of patients.<br>4 Receive good quality of teaching. |
| Evidence | From the handbook issued to students at the start of their attachment. |
| Staff involved | Audit facilitator and psychiatrist. |
| Sample | 32 students attached to service during academic year. |
| Data collection | Anonymous questionnaire. |
| Key findings | • Good quality of teaching experience and skills developed.<br>• Range of patients seen needs to be extended. |
| Feedback | All teachers involved. |
| Change | • Do a swap system with students attached to adult psychiatry. We tried a swap with adult placement students but this was only partially successful last year because of logistical problems of being on a different hospital site.<br>• Establish access to overdose assessment rota for our service. |
| Re-audit | Each year. |
| Resources used | 8 hours. |
| Notes | Problem making sure that the students completed and returned the questionnaire. It has a positive effect on teachers by enabling them to give quite detailed feedback, comments and suggestions. |
| Contact | Henry Rosenvinge, Southampton Community Health Services NHS Trust, Thornhill Unit, Moorgreen Hospital, Botley Road, West End, Southampton SO30 3JB. Tel: 01703 475 242; Fax: 01703 465 014. |

ORGANISATIONAL/ MANAGEMENT PROCESSES

# Appropriateness of placements on discharge from an old age psychiatry assessment unit

| | |
|---|---|
| Background | Core function of the unit. |
| Aims | 1 To improve clinical processes.<br>2 To assess reliability of assessment and case review process in placing patients. |
| Standards | Suitability of placement measured by client's needs still being met 3 months after move. |
| Evidence | Local consensus. |
| Staff involved | Registrar, charge nurse. |
| Sample | 60 admissions over 6 months. |
| Data collection | Case note review. |
| Key findings | 90% of placements successful by criteria employed. |
| Feedback | To ward staff, colleagues in hospital, trust audit seminar. |
| Change | Feel results to be satisfactory but, since 1996, more delay in placing patients after review – worry that results will worsen – needs to be re-audited. Social work department taking longer to place people now. |
| Re-audit | Seeking funding to review at 6-monthly/annual intervals. |
| Resources used | 60 hours. |
| Notes | Difficulty in setting satisfactory standard or measure as there are many pertinent variables. |
| Contact | Dr Susan Logie, Tayside Primary Care NHS Trust, Sunnyside Royal Hospital, Hillside, Montrose  DD10 9JP. Tel: 01674 830 361; Fax: 01674 830 361 extension 251. |

# Delayed discharges from elderly mental illness wards

| | |
|---|---|
| Background | Earlier audit of waiting times for admission revealed the main reason for delay was bed-blocking due to delayed discharges. |
| Aims | 1 To improve organisational processes and use of resources.<br>2 To identify the number of delayed discharges.<br>3 To identify the reasons for delayed discharges. |
| Standards | No patient must have their discharge delayed (delay=>7 days from date ready for discharge to actual discharge). |
| Evidence | Local consensus, local discharge policy. |
| Staff involved | Medical and nursing staff. |
| Sample | 60 patients – discharges from one ward for functional and one ward for organic illness over 6 months. |
| Data collection | Data collection form attached to front of notes and information completed by nursing and medical staff. |
| Data analysis | Data analysed using Borland Paradox Relational Database. |
| Key findings | 32% of those with functional illness had a delayed discharge, as did 90% of those with organic illness. |
| Feedback | Reports sent to commissioners, social services and health authority. |
| Change | The care manager is now informed earlier in the admission process. Whether social services have acted on findings is not known. |
| Re-audit | New inter-agency discharge policy in 1998. Re-audit 1998/99. |
| Resources used | Form very simple – mainly dates. Audit staff time for analysis. |
| Notes | Get social services involved from the start in joint project. |
| Contact | Sylvia Warwick, Clinical Audit and Research Manager, Fair Mile Hospital, Wallingford, Oxon OX10 9HH. Tel: 01491 651 281; Fax: 01491 651 128. |

DISCHARGE

*Clinical audit in mental health services for elderly people*

# Sending of discharge summaries to general practitioners within 10 working days

| | |
|---|---|
| Aim | To ensure continuity of care from in-patient and day patient stays. |
| Standards | All discharge summaries must be sent to general practitioners within 10 working days. |
| Evidence | Standard was taken from core quality standards in the trust. |
| Staff involved | Team secretary and assistant psychologist. |
| Sample | 92 clients discharged over 9 months. |
| Data collection | A discharge book was introduced to record date of discharge, date the dictated summary was received and date the typed summary was sent out. |
| Key findings | The standard was met for 98.3% of recorded discharges in the first 5 months of the audit, 92% in the sixth month and for all discharges in the last 3 months. |
| Feedback | Monthly feedback during the audit was provided to the secretary and the audit group. |
| Change | The procedures are in place to continue to meet this standard. It is not clear whether the presence of a book is instrumental in ensuring that the summaries are completed on time. The audit group decided that the secretary will be asked whether she wishes to continue to use the book in the future. Each registrar needs to be aware of the standard. It is now agreed that the senior registrar will cover periods of sickness or leave for the registrar. This needs to form part of the induction process. |
| Re-audit | No. |
| Contact | Sara Turner, Psychology Department, South West London and St George's Mental Health NHS Trust, Springfield University Hospital, 61 Glenburnie Road, London SW17 7DJ. Tel: 020 8682 6249; Fax: 020 8682 6256. |

DISCHARGE

# Use of discharge check-lists for in-patients

| | |
|---|---|
| Background | A discharge check-list was introduced in 1996 to improve continuity from in-patient to community status. |
| Aim | To evaluate how frequently discharge check-lists are being completed. |
| Standards | The discharge check-list must be completed for all in-patients discharged from the ward. |
| Evidence | Not recorded. |
| Staff involved | Ward staff and assistant psychologist. |
| Sample | All patients discharged. |
| Data collection | From discharge check-lists in files. |
| Data analysis | Descriptive statistics. |
| Key findings | Overall, 83% of discharge check-lists were completed. |
| Change | The discharge check-list will still be routinely used. The process will not be re-audited but random spot checks will be made. |
| Re-audit | No. |
| Contact | Sara Turner, Psychology Department, South West London and St George's Mental Health NHS Trust, Springfield University Hospital, 61 Glenburnie Road, London SW17 7DJ. Tel: 020 8682 6249; Fax: 020 8682 6256. |

# References and further reading

AMERICAN PSYCHIATRIC ASSOCIATION (1997) Practice Guideline for the Treatment of Patients with Schizophrenia. Washington DC: American Psychiatric Association.

BALOGH, R., BOND, S., DUNN, J., ET AL (1996) Newcastle Clinical Audit Toolkit: Mental Health. Centre for Health Services Research, University of Newcastle upon Tyne.

BUTTERY, Y. (1995) The Development of Audit. Findings of a National Survey of Healthcare Provider Units in England. London: CASPE Research.

CLINICAL STANDARDS ADVISORY GROUP (1995) Schizophrenia – Volume 1. London: HMSO.

COLLEGE OF OCCUPATIONAL THERAPISTS (1998) Clinical Audit Information Pack. London: College of Occupational Therapists.

DENNIS, N. (1995) Consumer audit in the NHS. British Journal of Hospital Medicine, 53, 532–534.

DEPARTMENT OF HEALTH (1990) Medical Audit. Working Paper 6. London: DoH.

—— (1994) Clinical Audit in the Nursing and Therapy Professions. London: DoH.

—— (1994) Improving Care Through Clinical Audit: Proceedings of a One Day Conference on Clinical Audit for the Health Care Professions. London: DoH.

—— (1994) Clinical Audit in the Nursing and Therapy Professions. London: DoH.

—— (1994) Medical Audit in Primary Care: A Collation of Evaluation Projects 1991–1993. London: DoH.

—— (1996) Clinical Audit in the NHS. London: DoH.

—— (1997) A Handbook on the Mental Health of Older People. London: DoH.

DIXON, N. (1996) Good practice in clinical audit – a summary of selected literature to support criteria for clinical audit. In NCCA Clinical Audit Action Pack. A Practical Approach. London: National Centre for Clinical Audit.

EXWORTHY, M., STEINER, A. & BARNARD, S. (1996) The future of clinical audit: the outcomes of a consensus conference. Journal of Clinical Effectiveness, 1, 129–133.

FIRTH-COZENS, J. (1993) Audit in Mental Health Services. Hove, East Sussex: Lawrence Erlbaum.

FREEMAN, C. P. (ED) (1995) ECT Handbook. Council Report CR39. London: Royal College of Psychiatrists.

GAILEY, F. (1996) Clinical Audit Enabler: A Clinical Audit Resource Reference Guide. Edinburgh: Lothian Clinical Audit.

LELLIOTT, P. (1994) Clinical audit in psychiatry. Hospital Update, February, 82–91.

—— & AUDINI, B. (1996) An Audit Pack for Monitoring the Care Programme Approach. London: NHS Executive.

LORD, J. & LITTLEJOHNS, P. (1997) Evaluating healthcare policies: the case of clinical audit. British Medical Journal, 315, 668–671.

MACDONALD, A. J. D. (1997) ABC of mental health: mental health in old age. British Medical Journal, 315, 413–417.

MORRELL, C. & HARVEY, G. (1999) The Clinical Audit Handbook. Improving the Quality of Care. London: Harcourt Brace.

NORTH OF ENGLAND EVIDENCE BASED GUIDELINE DEVELOPMENT PROJECT (1997) The Primary Care Management of Dementia. Newcastle: University of Newcastle upon Tyne.

PATTIE, A. H. & GILLEARD, C. J. (1969) Clifton Assessment Procedures for the Elderly. London: Hodder and Stoughton.

PRIMARY HEALTH CARE CLINICAL AUDIT WORKING GROUP OF CLINICAL OUTCOMES GROUP & CLINICAL OUTCOMES GROUP (1994) Clinical Audit in Primary Care, pp. 1–62. London: DoH.

RAO, R. (1998) Documentation of vascular risk factors in vascular dementia. Psychiatric Bulletin, 22, 97–99.

RIORDAN, J. & MOCKLER, D. (1997) Clinical Audit in Mental Health. Towards a Multidisciplinary Approach. Chichester: John Wiley & Sons Ltd.

ROYAL COLLEGE OF PHYSICIANS & BRITISH GERIATRICS SOCIETY (1992) High Quality Long-Term Care for Elderly People: Guidelines and Audit Measures. London: Royal College of Physicians.

ROYAL COLLEGE OF PSYCHIATRISTS (1994) The General Hospital Management of Adult Deliberate Self-Harm. A Consensus Statement on Standards for Service Provision. Council Report CR32. London: Royal College of Psychiatrists.

WALSHE, K. (1995) Evaluating Clinical Audit: Past Lessons, Future Directions. London: Royal Society of Medicine Press.

—— & BENNETT, J. (1991) Guidelines on Medical Audit and Confidentiality. Brighton Health Authority/ South East Thames Regional Health Authority.

—— & COLES, J. (1993) Evaluating Audit. Developing a Framework. London: CASPE Research.

# Resources

**College Research Unit**
11 Grosvenor Crescent
London SW1X 7EE
Tel: 0171 235 2351
Fax: 0171 235 2954
Email: CRULondon@compuserve.com
Website: www.rcpsych.ac.uk/cru/crufs/htm
The College Research Unit's activities include coordinating national audits and producing information sheets, guidelines, bibliographies, evidence-base briefings and clinical audit publications.

**Centre for Evidence-Based Mental Health**
Department of Psychiatry
University of Oxford
Warneford Hospital
Oxford OX3 7JX
Tel: 01865 226 476
Fax: 01865 793 101
Website: www.cebmh.com

**Clinical Audit Association**
Room 46, Cleethorpes Centre
Jackson Place
Wilton Road
Humberston
North East Lincolnshire
DN36 4AS
Tel: 01472 210 682
Email: pmkent@the-caa-ltd.demon.co.uk
Website: www.the-caa-ltd.demon.co.uk

**The Clinical Governance Resource and Development Unit**
Department of General Practice and Primary Health Care
University of Leicester
Leicester General Hospital
Gwendolen Road
Leicester LE5 4PW
Tel: 0116 258 4873
Fax: 0116 258 4982
Email: cgrdu@le.ac.uk
Website: www.le.ac.uk/cgrdu

**Clinical Resource and Audit Group (CRAG)**
Room 153, St Andrew's House
Regent Road
Edinburgh EH1 3DG
Tel: 0131 244 2235
Fax: 0131 244 2989

**College of Occupational Therapists**
106–114 Borough High Street
London SE1 1LB
Tel: 0171 357 6480
Fax: 0171 450 2365
Website: www.cot.co.uk

**Community Practitioners and Health Visitors Association (CPHVA) Clinical Audit Database**
40 Bermondsey Street
London SE1 3UD
Tel: 0171 939 7000
Fax: 0171 403 2275

**King's Fund**
11–13 Cavendish Square
London W1M 0AN
Tel: 0171 307 2400
Fax: 0171 307 2801
Website: www.KingsFund.co.uk

**Pavilion Publishing**
8 St George's Place
Brighton
East Sussex
BN1 4GB
Tel: 01273 623222
Fax: 01273 625526
Email: pavpub@pavilion.co.uk
Website: www.pavpub.com

**Royal College of Nursing, Nursing and Midwifery Audit Information Service**
20 Cavendish Square
London W1M 0AB
Tel: 0171 647 3831
Fax: 0171 647 3437

**Royal College of Paediatrics and Child Health**
50 Hallam Street
London W1N 6DE
Tel: 0171 307 5600
fax: 0171 307 5601
Email: enquiries@rcpch.ac.uk

**Royal College of Speech and Language Therapists**
7 Bath Place
Rivington Street
London EC2A 3SU
Tel: 0171 613 3855
Fax: 0171 613 3854

# Project submission form

If you have any clinical audit projects you would like included in future editions of this book, please copy and complete this form and return it to:

Kirsty MacLean Steel
Royal College of Psychiatrists' Research Unit
11 Grosvenor Crescent
London SW1X 7EE

---

**Name:** _____

**Address:** _____

_____

**Telephone:** _____     _____

**Email:** _____

**Clinician responsible for audit (if different from above):** _____

**Date of audit (year) and period of time over which data were collected:**

_____

---

Notes about the completion of form: please continue on separate sheet if necessary and attach your audit report to refer to if this is easier. If you have any questions regarding the information requested on this form, please contact Kirsty MacLean Steel or Claire Palmer on 0171 235 2351, ext. 282.

| **Clinical audit project title** | |
|---|---|
| **Background** Why was this audit considered important (i.e. why was this topic selected)? | |
| **Aims and objectives** Did the audit aim to improve (please tick more than one if appropriate): | (a) clinical processes (e.g. assessment, treatment) ☐<br>(b) organisational processes (e.g. waiting times, information recording) ☐<br>(c) health outcomes ☐<br>(d) service user or carer satisfaction with service ☐<br>(e) the use of resources ☐ |

| **Standards** Did you set explicit, measurable standards against which practice could be compared? Please outline: | Standard 1: _____<br><br>Standard 2: _____<br><br>Standard 3: _____<br><br>Standard 4: _____<br><br>Standard 5: _____ |
|---|---|
| On what were the standards based, e.g. local consensus, research evidence, national guidelines, feedback from service users etc.? | |
| **Involvement** Who was involved in the audit? | |
| **Assessing practice against the standards** What was the sample size and how was it selected?<br><br>How were the data collected?<br><br>How were the data analysed? | |
| **Key findings** | |
| **Feedback of findings** To whom were the results of the study communicated and how? | |

*Clinical audit in mental health services for elderly people*

| | |
|---|---|
| **Suggestions for change**<br><br>Following the audit have you come up with suggestions for changes in practice?<br><br>If so, what are they?<br><br>If not, why not? | |
| **Changing practice**<br><br>Have there been any significant things which have either helped, or prevented, change from being implemented? Please describe. | |
| **Re-audit**<br><br>After how long do you plan to re-audit? | |
| **Resources**<br><br>Approximately how much staff time was taken to complete the audit cycle (hours)?<br><br>Were any other costs or resources needed? | |
| **Evaluating the audit**<br><br>What problems did you encounter (if any) in undertaking the audit?<br><br>If you were doing this project again, are there any aspects of the audit you would change? | |
| What advice would you offer to someone attempting a similar audit? | |

LIBRARY AND INFORMATION SERVICE
YORK DISTRICT HOSPITAL
YORK
YO31 8HE